How to Buy or Sell Your Home in a Changing Market

How to Buy or Sell Your Home in a Changing Market

Warren Boroson

Medical Economics Books
Oradell, New Jersey 07649

Library of Congress Cataloging in Publication Data

Boroson, Warren.
   How to buy or sell your home in a changing market.

   Includes index.
   1. House buying—United States.   2. House selling—United States.   I. Title.
HD1379.B644   1983   643′.12   82-14339
ISBN 0-87489-278-3

Cover design by Douglas Steel

ISBN 0-87489-278-3

Medical Economics Company Inc.
Oradell, New Jersey 07649

Printed in the United States of America

Copyright © 1983 by Medical Economics Company Inc., Oradell, N.J. 07649. All rights reserved. None of the content of this publication may be reproduced, stored in a retrieval system, or transmitted in any form or by any means (electronic, mechanical, photocopying, recording, or otherwise) without the prior written permission of the publisher.

*To my parents,
Henry and Cecelia Boroson*

CONTENTS

Foreword   *ix*

Preface   *xi*

Publisher's Notes   *xiii*

Introduction   *xiv*

I OWNING & BUYING

1 Will Your House Be Worth a King's Ransom in A.D. 1990?   *3*

2 Newfangled Mortgages and Creative Financing   *9*

3 Dirty Tricks Some Brokers Play   *25*

4 How to Haggle for Fun and Profit   *35*

5 Surprising Facts About Homeowners Insurance   *41*

6 Measuring the Tax Angles   *59*

II OWNING

7 Smart and Dumb Home Improvements   *69*

8 How to Trap a Homing Pigeon   *75*

9 Three Ways to Knock Down a Broker's Commission   *85*

| 10 | The Compleat Guide to Selling It Yourself | *89* |
| 11 | The Hard-to-Sell House | *99* |

III BUYING

12	The Best Cities to Live In—and the Worst	*107*
13	Everyone's Dream: The Custom-Built House	*119*
14	The Search for a Real Creampuff	*129*
15	Pay a Broker to Find You a House?	*141*
16	The Continuing Scandal of Closing Costs	*145*
17	The Perils of Buying a Mansion	*159*
18	Condomania	*167*
19	Is a Vacation Home a Shrewd Investment?	*175*
20	The Whole Truth About Time-Sharing	*179*
21	How to Tell Whether a House Is Well Built	*185*
22	Housebreaking Your Septic Tank	*193*
23	The Retirement Spot That's Best for You	*201*

Appendix: A Concise Guide to the New Mortgages   *210*

Glossary   *213*

Index   *223*

FOREWORD

The subject of private homes is so vast that it would take an encyclopedia to really cover it completely.

Despite the vastness of the subject, *How to Buy or Sell Your Home in a Changing Market* does a fine job of hitting the high points. It manages to cover an awesome amount of territory—not just buying and selling houses, but creative financing, condominiums and co-operatives, time-sharing, taxes, vacation homes, and more.

The author's prejudices, I am happy to report, usually coincide with my own. In particular, he hammers home what I consider the single best piece of advice you can furnish any homebuyer or seller: Give special care to choosing the people you hire. Your ultimate success in buying, selling, or building a house depends to a tremendous extent on the quality of those you consult.

Boroson not only covers the subject so well, he does it without pulling any punches. The book does a good job of pointing out the pitfalls and dangers. (Sensitive real-estate agents, be forewarned.) The world of real estate is still very much a place where the buyer, and the seller, must beware. In my own experience, half the people signing contracts have no idea what they are signing.

Some chapters, it is true, are written in an amusing style. But in retrospect, perhaps it's that style that helps make the book so easy to read and such a pleasure to polish off. I think it was the Latin poet Horace who said that all good literature is both *dulce et utile*—that is, sweet and useful. This book amply fills the bill.

Sidney Goldstone, M.D.

PREFACE

This book is intended to be as up-to-date as possible, to help both buyers and sellers cope with the current, radically changing housing market.

Today's homeowners may be more eager to improve their houses than to sell out and lose their deliciously low interest rates; or, if they are of a mind to sell, they may be constrained to assist buyers with the financing; and even if they are willing to sell their houses at a loss, they may find buyers as scarce as G-rated movies.

Today's buyers may be frustrated in trying to get mortgage money, or discouraged by grotesquely high interest rates, or bewildered by having to choose among the vast array of puzzling new mortgages.

Chapter 2 tells how to choose among the newfangled mortgages, how to scrape up mortgage money in general, and how both buyer and seller can avoid being burned by creative financing. The first chapter takes a hard look at houses as investments, now that the recent miserable housing market has produced justifiable doubts. A later chapter offers guidelines on choosing improvements that will raise the value of a house—taking into consideration the increasing cost of energy, the new tax laws, and changing public preferences and tastes.

Also in keeping with the effort to be up-to-date, there are chapters on the pros and cons of time-sharing, on how to buy and sell condominiums and co-operatives, and on evaluating that curious creature who has quietly slipped on stage, the buyer-broker.

Another purpose of this book is to help people buy and sell *expensive* houses, which present special gnarly difficulties. An expensive house is defined as any residence significantly more costly than others in the same area. Of course, there is advice for people looking to buy or sell modest homes, too. Chapters 7 through 11 are mainly for sellers, chapters 12 through 23 focus on the buyer.

This book is also intended to be forthright. Many other books on residential real estate are so sugary that they could have been titled *Dick and Jane Buy Their First House.* In reality it's a cutthroat business, haunted by late 19th-century ethical standards. Buyer is pitted against seller; real-estate agent against buyer (and sometimes seller, too); lawyer, sometimes, against his own client. The best attitude is one of watchful wariness. If this book seems unduly harsh on real-estate agents, lawyers, architects, title-insurance companies, contractors and subcontractors, it's only that these things had to be said at length here because so little is said elsewhere.

Finally, this book attempts to be good journalism. Instead of surveying the complex world of residential real estate from the purview of one real-estate agent in one county of the United States, I have—wherever possible—turned to polls and surveys, and to the experiences and views of a battery of brokers, architects, lawyers, house inspectors, lenders, government officials, accountants, and so forth.

Certain individuals deserve special thanks for their help: M. A. Libien, C.P.A.; William J. Ward, A.I.A.; John Faulkner, broker; Hal Goodman, who edited the manuscript and insisted, in the interest of readability, on the use of the masculine pronoun to include both sexes; and my wife, Rebecca, a professional lexicographer, who prepared the Glossary.

Readers are invited to send in their comments.

Warren Boroson

PUBLISHER'S NOTES

About the author: A licensed real-estate salesman, Warren Boroson has published articles in such magazines as *The New York Times Magazine, Reader's Digest, Better Homes and Gardens, Family Circle, Woman's Day, Travel & Leisure, TV Guide,* the *New York News Sunday Magazine, Mechanix Illustrated, RF Illustrated, across the board,* and *Mainliner.* An honors graduate of Columbia College, New York City, Mr. Boroson has worked on the staff of *Money* magazine and is currently a senior editor with *Medical Economics* magazine. He teaches a course on buying and selling houses at Bergen Community College, Paramus, N.J. He and his wife and their two children, Bram, 14, and Matthew, 12, live in Glen Rock, N.J.

Sidney Goldstone, M.D., author of the Foreword, is a family practitioner in Gary, Ind., who has run his own construction company and built some 400 houses.

W. Robert Felix Jr., M.D., who wrote the Introduction, is assistant professor of surgery at Harvard Medical School and has held a real-estate license since 1968. His wife is a full-time broker.

INTRODUCTION

The statement "Invest in real estate because it will always grow" has been excellent advice for many years. A steady increase in value of about 10 percent a year in equity, and a sizable tax savings each year, have been the rule.

But as this book goes to press, the residential real-estate market is recovering from its worst slump since the Great Depression. The slump was due to powerful economic factors: high interest rates, the demise of many savings and loan institutions, and the reduced availability of mortgage money.

Even so, house prices still reflect a long-term 10-percent-a-year increase, and real estate remains a good investment so long as you don't need liquidity. There just isn't the turnover we had become accustomed to in the late '60s and early '70s.

In Warren Boroson's book we are treated to a delightful collection of sound advice sprinkled with a liberal amount of anecdotes and personal experiences. Mr. Boroson's style is very readable, informative, and full of wit. There is solid advice on how to buy and sell your own home and how to avoid unscrupulous real-estate agents. The model checklists and fact sheets and the special records, not familiar to the average homeowner, are innovative, and, I am sure, useful. Especially important, in this time of high mortgage rates, is the advice on how to qualify a prospective buyer.

Chapter 15, "Pay a Broker to Find You a House?," deserves special attention. The idea is intriguing. Currently, the seller pays the broker's commission. The broker, therefore, works harder to sell his own listings and to get as high a price as possible for the seller's property. The current system doesn't always work to the buyer's advantage. But brokers don't like this system, either. They often work long, uncompensated hours with a potential buyer, only to learn later that the buyer purchased a home through another agent.

Paying a broker to find you a home is a very satisfying idea. The broker is stimulated to work diligently for the buyer whether he is receiving a flat fee, an hourly rate, or a percentage of the asking price. The last method of compensation has the greatest appeal to me, but it doesn't protect the broker from fickle buyers.

Whatever method of compensation is agreed upon in a buyer-broker contract, sellers should understand that they are in a different ball game when dealing with a broker who is truly working for a buyer. It is probably best, as suggested in this book, for brokers to decide which side they are on in any given situation. This approach will avoid untenable conflicts of interest. At present, I believe this idea will work best when a broker represents a buyer in a for-sale-by-owner situation. Everyone profits. The buyer gets a desirable home at the best (lowest) price, and the broker gets an equitable commission for all his time and effort on behalf of the buyer, and without having had to push his own listings to do it.

Chapter 3, "Dirty Tricks Some Brokers Play," is entertaining and informative. But the reader should know that almost all of the dirty tricks listed are cause for loss of license in most states. Very few brokers will engage in these kinds of activities. People who do not hold real-estate agents in high esteem are quick to complain to their lawyers. They, in turn, should in good conscience suggest that a complaint be filed with the local real-estate board. Competition is so keen in this business that brokers themselves are quick to recommend that complaints be filed with the board about other brokers. After all, this keeps the profession clean, and sometimes cuts down on the competition.

Chapter 13, on custom-built houses, is another gem. Mr. Boroson's warnings are right on the mark. From my own experience, I wholeheartedly endorse several of his important points. The Home Owners Warranty should be supplied by every builder. Bonds to guarantee payment of subcontractors are also needed. Proper insulation should be guaranteed. (Building codes usually address only electrical and plumbing standards.) The bonus/penalty provision for early or late completion of the job is an excellent way to encourage the builder to constantly work in your interest.

Mr. Boroson has put together an enlightening, useful, factual, and—at times—amusing book about a subject very important to nearly all of us at one time or another. Our homes represent the largest investment many of us will ever make. This book should help make buying a home a wise and painless investment and selling that home a profitable venture.

W. Robert Felix Jr., M.D.

OWNING & BUYING

CHAPTER

1 WILL YOUR HOUSE BE WORTH A KING'S RANSOM IN A.D. 1990?

By 1990, the residential housing scene in this country may be markedly different. The changes possibly in store should color your present-day thoughts about where to live, what kind of house to buy, what improvements to make and not to make, what sort of house to cling to and what sort of house to be in something of a hurry to unload.

THE LAST GREAT COLLECTIBLE?
Most authorities agree that, purely as an investment, the American house—especially the detached house in the isolated suburbs—has seen its glory days. As investments, houses now cost more to buy and more to run, and they return less. They are no longer the all-time, A-No. 1, super-duper inflation hedge.

George Sternlieb, director of the Center for Urban Policy Research at Rutgers University in New Jersey, gloomily declares: "The detached house as an investment vehicle is finished. The Age of Collectibles is over. Diamonds aren't what they used to be, beer cans aren't so good, and housing—the last of the great collectibles—is dead."

Near the other end of the spectrum, Anthony Downs, a senior fellow at the Brookings Institution in Washington, D.C., sees the suburban house as "still a reasonably good investment for the 1980s. It's going to be better than the bond market, and maybe better than the stock market." Houses have usually fared well during inflationary times, Downs points out, and the era of inflation isn't over yet.

THE BIG SIX
Whether private housing becomes a poor investment or a reasonably good investment, it is clear that the roots of change number at least six:

1. *Mortgage rates have soared and will remain high.* Time was when Uncle Sam saw to it that lenders obtained money for mortgages very cheaply, and could lend mortgage money fairly cheaply. Now money is no longer cheap. True, the banks' money market deposit accounts and the new Individual Retirement Accounts have made mortgage money plentiful. But the cost of borrowing will surely remain high. And with growing economic prosperity along with government military spending, the cost of borrowing money may climb.

2. *The cost of running a house will continue to soar.* Not just the costs involved with heating and cooling, but also the costs of water, of lawn fertilizer, of repairs, of electricity, and so on. Not long ago, homeowners typically spent 25 percent of their incomes on housing. Now most spend one-third of their incomes, and some spend 40 percent or more. "At projected price levels," writes Bruce Stoker, a senior researcher at the Worldwatch Institute, "it will not be uncommon for people to spend half their incomes on shelter."

3. *Commuting costs will climb.* This includes the cost of driving to work yourself as well as using mass transportation (the government is cutting back its support). The rising cost of commuting will tighten the screws on suburbanites living far from their places of employment. And although more and more people will start working at home, they won't number enough to make a significant difference.

4. *Houses are no longer seen as the Perfect Investment.* In the clutch, the housing market collapsed like, well, so many houses of cards. People won't forget.

5. As it is, *house prices have risen out of the range of most first-time buyers*. The relatively stagnant housing market has been giving the incomes of first-time buyers a chance to catch up with typical house prices (now close to $70,000). But this

cohort of latecomers will always be unable to afford as much in the way of housing as previous cohorts.

6. *There should continue to be a strong demand for private housing.* Apartments are expected to remain scarce and rentals high over the remainder of the decade.

Yet an increasing number of people will be seeking shelter, because the number of singles and divorced in the population will go up. The Harvard-MIT Joint Center for Urban Studies estimates that, by 1990, households consisting of unattached people—the single, the divorced, the widowed—will equal households consisting of married couples.

Besides, during this decade the Baby Boom generation— 42 million strong—will be entering their 30s, traditionally the age when people want private housing.

The upshot is that the demand for affordable private housing should be fierce.

CONSEQUENCES
Given these trends, we can predict that:

• *The relatively high-cost, high-maintenance house will be consigned to the doghouse.*
The residence to be wary of is a sprawling, energy-inefficient ranch house, with five or more bedrooms, way out in the hinterlands. It may not turn into the equivalent of an elephantine, eight-mile-a-gallon, old-time Buick, but it is not going to quicken the pulses of very many would-be buyers.

The sprawling five-bedroom house won't become a dodo. Some large houses will twin, the way big, fat movie theaters have given birth. The young will live with the old; friends will move in with friends. If zoning ordinances aren't relaxed, they will be ignored.

In any case, we Americans aren't so sweetly reasonable that we will just turn our backs on big houses. Roominess, to most Americans, will always be next to godliness. If all Americans were sweetly reasonable, by now we would be pedaling bicycles to work instead of driving cars. Downs predicts that "houses with four or five bedrooms might decline relative to other units, but the market for them isn't going to collapse."

• *If the moderately expensive house is in the doghouse, the low-cost, low-maintenance house will be, of course, in the catbird seat.*

Not just condominiums, townhouses, and duplexes, but detached houses with just two bedrooms, combined living rooms and dining rooms, and tiny yards. They will be cheaper to buy, cheaper to run. And the smaller living space will suit our new demographic needs—more elderly people in the population, more families with few children. "The wave of the future," says Sternlieb, "is the lower house standard." On the West Coast, he notes, already 40 percent of all housing being purchased has only two bedrooms. "And to a very substantial degree, the West Coast is the fashion center of America."

While Anthony Downs doubts that there will be an acute shortage of housing, he does grant that the two-bedroom house will become more popular. "It used to be a dog," he says, "and now it's going to get less doggy."

• *Luxury houses—say, $200,000 and up—will continue to prosper.*

Ritzy five-bedroom houses in Palm Beach will still be sought after. There's an awesome number of fabulously rich people in this country and abroad, and they will keep on pampering themselves. Only in energy-starved New England, reports Charles H. Seilheimer Jr., president of the Sotheby Parke Bernet International Realty Corporation, which specializes in luxury houses, do prospective buyers of 15-room mansions remember to inquire about heating costs.

In sum, the housing market of the future may resemble a U. There will be a demand for modest housing and for mansions; the market for what lies in between may droop. Toyotas and Mercedes will be up, Chevys down.

• *Distant suburbs—unless they are the lordly preserves of the very rich—will suffer.*

No, suburbs in general won't sink into Siberia. The cost of commuting to work won't be exorbitant in most suburbs because so many businesses have already moved nearby. Besides, most people will turn their thermostats down and drive rinky-dink cars rather than do anything so drastic as moving back to the Bronx. Downs says that Brookings has done intensive analyses of the consequences of high energy costs, and "generally only the farthest-out communities will suffer a slowdown and decline in relative attractiveness."

• *The second-home market will slump.*

Only recreational houses in the choicest locations—the sort that people are dying to rent—should appreciate much.

For most people, running just one house will be onerous enough. And time-sharing (see Chapter 20) can take care of their vacation needs rather cheaply.

• *Creative financing—the seller helps out the buyer—will become a permanent feature of the landscape.*

Fortunately, it will become safer, too. More and more commonly, these private mortgages are being insured against default. Right now creative financing is in abeyance. It may come back with a roar if interest rates climb.

SUMMING UP

All these forecasts shouldn't panic any homeowner or homebuyer. As Gwendolyn Wright, an architectural historian, states in her book *Building the Dream: A Social History of American Housing* (1981), the "contemporary crisis is neither unprecedented nor as devastating as it seems." Americans will adjust; the housing market will endure.

But there are certain obvious lessons to be learned.

Stop sneering at two-bedroom houses. Be dubious about tacking on a fourth or fifth bedroom to a house you own. If your nest egg is small, hold off buying that cottage in the backwoods. If your five-bedroom ranch in outer suburbia constitutes most of your worldly wealth, plan to sell it sooner rather than later. Don't automatically buy up into a roomier house for investment purposes. And bone up on creative financing—the subject of the next chapter.

The paramount lesson is that you should surrender any lingering expectations that a house will help you get rich quick. In 1990, sad to say, your house very probably will *not* be worth a king's ransom.

But you should ask yourself what you want a pile of money for, if not to lead the Good Life. Ask yourself whether the place where you live, eat, sleep, play, brush your teeth, read, listen to music, hold wild parties, and watch too much television shouldn't be reasonably opulent.

Says Ken Kerin, an economist for the National Association of Realtors: "We've gone a little bit astray when we think of homes as investments instead of places to live. We go through life only once, and we should have a place that accommodates our way of life as best we can afford."

Says Anthony Downs, similarly: "I don't think fairly well-to-do people should give a damn whether they make any money on their houses. The average doctor, lawyer, engineer, accountant, or executive doesn't have to think of his home as a means of capital appreciation. It's not immoral to think of your house as an investment, but it shouldn't be your primary concern. If you are going to spend a lot of time in your house, you should enjoy the time you spend there."

In short, homeowners in A.D. 1990 should be happy to settle for a mere prince's ransom.

CHAPTER

2 NEWFANGLED MORTGAGES AND CREATIVE FINANCING

Before we delve into (1) shopping for a newfangled mortgage, (2) shopping for any old mortgage, and (3) creative financing, let's have a little innocent fun. By means of a tricky quiz.

TEST YOUR MORTGAGE MASTERY*
1. The buyer of your house wants to assume your low-interest mortgage. You have no reason to be anything but overjoyed.

☐ true ☐ false

Answer: *False. Having an assumable mortgage certainly can help you sell your house, as well as spare you a possible charge for paying off your loan before its normal term. But if the buyer defaults, you can still be held responsible for the debt. It's possible to draw up a contract freeing you from further responsibility, with the lender's approval, but few sellers do.*

2. If your mortgage has a due-on-sale clause, you must pay the lender the balance of the mortgage when you sell. Your balance cannot be assumed by a buyer.

☐ true ☐ false ☐ not necessarily

Answer: *Not necessarily. Due-on-sale clauses in mortgage contracts* apart from those from federal savings and loan associations *may not*

---

* Reprinted in part from the October 1977 issue of *Money* magazine by special permission; © 1977, Time Inc.

be legally enforceable in 14 states—*Arizona, California, Colorado, Florida, Georgia, Illinois, Iowa, Michigan, Mississippi, New Mexico, Ohio, South Carolina, Utah, and Washington. Such clauses in mortgages from federal savings and loan associations are exceptions because the Supreme Court has upheld their enforceability, despite any state decisions to the contrary. Would-be buyers and sellers in those 14 states would be wise to take action pronto, because mortgages from other lenders are expected to have their due-on-sale clauses also made enforceable soon.*

3. You obtain a 30-year mortgage for $65,000. The monthly sum of principal plus interest is $800. How much interest will you wind up paying? **A.** You can't tell without knowing the interest rate. **B.** $223,000.

Answer: *B. The total of the principal you repay is $65,000. So multiply $800 by 12 (months) by 30 (years) and then subtract $65,000.*

4. You obtain a mortgage, and you make no down payment on it. Obviously, you must therefore be: **A.** Rich. **B.** A banker. **C.** A veteran.

Answer: *C. Only loans guaranteed by the Veterans Administration require no down payment.*

5. May a nonveteran assume a veteran's mortgage that has been guaranteed by the VA?

☐ yes ☐ no

Answer: *Yes.*

6. Families that default on their mortgages tend to have five or more dependents.

☐ true ☐ false

Answer: *True, according to a study in Connecticut. They also tend to have other debts besides the mortgage, and a mortgage loan that is large relative to the value of the house. Most defaults occur during the first five years of a mortgage, probably because the families don't yet have much money invested in the house.*

7. A mortgage borrower defaults. The mortgage lender forecloses and sells the property. Amount due: $80,000. Amount realized: $90,000. Who gets the extra $10,000?

☐ borrower ☐ lender

Answer: *Borrower.*

8. Private mortgage insurance protects the lender in case the borrower defaults. With such insurance, the down payment may be as low as: **A.** 5 percent. **B.** 10 percent. **C.** 15 percent of the price of the house.

Answer: *A.*

9. If your mortgage is insured by the Federal Housing Administration, your house may cost: **A.** Around $70,000. **B.** Around $100,000. **C.** No limit.

Answer: *C. On an FHA-insured mortgage, the sale price is unlimited. But the FHA will insure only 97 percent of the first $25,000 of a mortgage, and 95 percent of the remainder, up to $70,000 or so (the amount varies in different states) on a one-family house.*

10. If you fall behind on your mortgage payments, you may not legally sell your house.

☐ true ☐ false

Answer: *False. But either you or your buyer must make up the deficit.*

THOSE NEWFANGLED MORTGAGES

A while back, Thomas Lee, a young intern in Boston who wanted to buy a condominium, was turned down twice for a fixed-rate mortgage. So he tried to get a mortgage by co-applying with his father, a professor at the Massachusetts Institute of Technology. And if any newfangled mortgage became available, Lee swore he would pounce on it.

Dr. Lee should have reconsidered. The fact is that if you're shopping for a home, you should try to avoid the new floating-rate mortgages and get the traditional fixed-rate mortgage, provided that its rate isn't bloated out of sight. After all, the fixed-rate mortgage is immune to inflation. And in the event of a sharp deflation (interest rates go, say, 2 points lower), it may be worth your while to pay off the mortgage—despite any prepayment penalty or loan-origination costs—and get a new one. Another plus: With a fixed-rate mortgage, you know from month to month what payment you will be hit with. In the words of Thomas L. O'Dea, a real-estate consultant in Winston-Salem, N.C., "It's the devil you *know.*"

In the confusing marketplace of new mortgages, in fact, you should generally select one on the basis of how closely it resembles the borrower's old friend, the fixed-rate mortgage. In the Appendix is a concise description of these new mortgages.

A graduated-payment mortgage (GPM) can be the closest thing to a fixed-rate mortgage. Although GPMs are being issued with floating rates now, some still have interest rates that are fixed over the life of the loan.

Still, the amount of the monthly payment of a GPM will change over the years. For the first year, payments are abnormally low. For the next five years, payments go up. When they level off, the payments are higher than for a comparable fixed-rate mortgage.

A GPM may be appropriate for a young family just starting out on the Yellow Brick Road to success. As their income increases, they can better afford the higher mortgage payments. But a drawback is that the low early payments may not be sufficient to pay all the interest due. After a few years of payments, a homeowner may owe more than he did when he started out.

Also, the GPM may be an endangered species. Before too long it may be wiped out by the floating-rate graduated-payment mortgage.

Floating-rate mortgages. In the best of all possible worlds, as someone has said, all borrowers would have fixed-rate mortgages and all lenders would have floating-rate mortgages. The interest rate of such a mortgage fluctuates according to a preselected economic index, such as the interest rate on five-year Treasury obligations.

The whole purpose of floating-rate mortgages, of course, is to protect the lender against galloping inflation. Lenders have to pay dearly these days to get money to parcel out, and they are stuck with a bunch of old, low-paying mortgages. Some lucky homeowners are still holding on to 5½ percent mortgages.

There's a flock of very peculiar lending institutions around, and there's a flock of very peculiar floating-rate mortgages. But most authorities are convinced that the Big Two are destined to be:

1. the *adjustable mortgage loan* (AML), offered by federally chartered S&Ls and savings banks, and
2. the *adjustable-rate mortgage* (ARM), offered by federally chartered commercial banks.

If the interest rate on a floating-rate mortgage is much lower than the rate on any fixed-rate mortgage you are offered, consider opting for the former. But only if the interest rate on the floating-rate mortgage is likely to remain stable over the years.

Look for a floating-rate mortgage that has—as Roger Harrison, a financial consultant in Norman, Okla., puts it—"all sorts of bells and whistles on it." He's talking, of course, about limitations on:

- how often the interest rate can change,
- how much it can change each time, and
- the total change permitted over the life of the loan.

Also check which interest-rate index triggers any movement in the mortgage's rate. By and large, the longer the term of the index used, the less risky it is. That's why a rate pegged to the rate on five-year Treasury obligations is desirable.

Least desirable are indexes that are likely to head higher, and soon. Example: a national or regional average of the rates that savings and loan associations pay to raise money. The reason is that federal regulators have let S&Ls raise the rates they may pay on money. Also be leery of state-chartered S&Ls that use as an index their own costs of borrowing. That allows an S&L to borrow money at whatever rate it chooses, then simply pass along the charge to borrowers.

Renegotiable and rollover mortgages. Cousins of the floating-rate mortgage are renegotiable mortgages and rollover mortgages, which have their interest rates adjusted every five years or so. If the lender *must* renew the loan, and if there's a limit on how much the interest rate can go up, these mortgages are not bad. But such mortgages are fading away in this country.

Growing equity mortgages. A new entry into the field is Merrill Lynch's growing equity mortgage. For the first year, the mortgage payments are based on an interest rate pegged 2 to 3 points below the market rate. After the first year, the payments will fluctuate according to a U.S. Commerce Department index of disposable income per capita. But any rise in the payments would go toward reducing only the *principal,* not the interest. This means that such a mortgage can be paid off in a mere 10 or 11 years. Ingenious and promising.

Shared-appreciation mortgages. A dark horse is the shared-appreciation mortgage. The lender lowers his interest rate—or helps with the down payment—in return for a slice of the action, namely, a percentage of the house's future appreciation. "If you're trying to build an estate," says Alan Crittenden of Nevada City, Calif., a leading publisher of real-estate literature, "this is no way to do it."

Clearly, choosing the best mortgage these days can be a formidable job. What if you are offered a choice between:

- a fixed-rate mortgage with a very high interest rate;
- a floating-rate mortgage with a moderate interest rate and all sorts of limits on how high and how fast it can rise; and
- a floating-rate mortgage with a very low interest rate but with hardly any limits on how high and how fast it can rise?

Answer: This is precisely the reason that God created accountants.

THE PERFECT MORTGAGE
There is, alas, a lot more to shopping for a mortgage, whether it's newfangled or not.

First: the down payment. The old rule was to get the smallest down payment and the longest term. Reasons:

- When you came to sell, your mortgage balance would still be substantial, and buyers would be eager to assume it because of its low interest rate.
- With a low down payment in relation to the price of the house, you could afford a more expensive house.
- The interest you owed, all in all, might be staggering, but it would be tax-deductible.

NEWFANGLED MORTGAGES AND CREATIVE FINANCING

• With all your spare money, you could move into other lucrative investments.

• Naturally, you would also be paying off the mortgage, as the years passed, with dollars cheapened by inflation.

Now that mortgage rates are so high, and so many mortgages have floating interest rates, some of the old rules no longer apply. If you are paying 12 or 13 percent on a mortgage, even recognizing that the interest is deductible, you will have to search far and wide to find an investment that pays more. Besides, a high down payment may persuade a lender to lower his interest rate. Thus, it boils down to this: Do you have a better use for your money than using it to reduce monthly principal and interest, and possibly the interest rate?

If a small down payment is all you want to make, or all you can afford, consider private mortgage insurance. In fact, many lenders will insist on it if you pay less than 20 percent down. Usually private mortgage insurance costs 1 percent of the mortgage, payable at the closing, and ¼ percent of the outstanding balance in succeeding years—usually 10 years.

These days, the length of the loan is no big deal. The monthly payment on a 20-year mortgage may not be much higher than it would be on a 30-year mortgage, interest rates being what they are. Ask your lender to figure the differences in monthly payments between mortgages of varying terms.

But, even today, look for a loan with no penalty if you pay it off early (should you move, say), or at least a penalty of only a few hundred dollars that applies only during the first few years of the life of the mortgage.

Try to avoid a mortgage with an acceleration clause, whereby the lender can demand all of his money back if you break one of a list of rules, such as making a late payment.

Avoid extra charges wherever possible, such as loan-origination fees and—heaven forbid!—mortgage life insurance. If you have adequate life insurance, you just don't need it.

One point equals 1 percent of the mortgage. When interest rates are at the 12 and 13 percent levels, six points are equivalent to about 1 percent of interest.

Some lenders collect money from you in an escrow account to pay for property taxes and home insurance. "I appreciate their doing the work," says Ellis M. Fribush, M.D., a cardiologist in Pittsfield, Mass., who is unusually knowledgeable about

EXHIBIT 2-1

COMPARING MORTGAGE OFFERS

If you're going mortgage-hunting, use the worksheet below to compare offers. Ideally, look for a fixed-rate mortgage without an astronomical interest rate. Failing that, look for a floating-rate mortgage with an interest rate that will be especially stable. Decide for yourself what you want in the way of a down payment. The term doesn't matter much anymore. Try to avoid points (loan charges, each equal to 1 percent of the mortgage), loan fees, prepayment penalties, and acceleration clauses. Try to earn interest on the home insurance and property taxes that the lender may collect from you—"escrow with interest."

Lender	1	2	3
Name, phone			
Loan amount			
Down payment			
Term			
Interest rate			
Interest type (fixed, ARM, etc.)			
Frequency of rate changes			
Limit on single changes			
Limit on total changes			
Interest-rate index			
Points			
Loan fees			
Mortgage insurance?			
Prepayment penalty?			
Acceleration clause?			
Escrow with interest?			

mortgages. "But I'd be happier if they paid me interest on the money they hold, as they are required to do in a few states."

In searching for the perfect mortgage, don't put everything into the hands of a real-estate agent. Says Dr. Fribush, "Brokers have connections, but no one is as interested in saving you money as you are. When I was mortgage-shopping, I visited all three savings and loan associations and both commercial banks in my community, as well as one S&L out of town. And it was well worth it in terms of the money I saved."

WHERE TO SHOP
Visit all sorts of different lending institutions. Try mortgage companies and S&Ls, but nowadays commercial banks are your best bet. Check your Yellow Pages under "Mortgages," "Real-estate loans," or "Trust deeds," to find out who's lending. Visit some places in town, some places out of town. I myself live in Glen Rock, N.J., and my mortgagee is in Brooklyn, N.Y. Naturally, zero in on institutions where you normally do business; as a customer, you may be treated more graciously.

Try a federal or state credit union, too. In some areas—the Midwest and New England, for example—there are "community-based" credit unions. You can join without belonging to a company that has such a union. Not many credit unions offer mortgages, and when they do, it's only on houses that are not more than 150 percent more expensive than the average price of houses in the area. But the interest rate on credit-union mortgages will probably be competitive. And credit unions pay interest on money held in escrow for property taxes.

One clever tactic you should try is asking the seller which lender holds his mortgage. Then call the lender and ask whether the mortgage has been purchased by the Federal National Mortgage Association. Fannie Mae frequently buys mortgages from institutional lenders without the borrower's ever knowing about it. If Fannie Mae does hold the mortgage, it may give you a new mortgage for a few points below the market rates. The arrangements will be made by the lender, though, not by Fannie Mae.

If the seller's mortgage is nonassumable but it has been sold to the Federal Home Loan Mortgage Association (Freddie Mac), by the way, you can now assume it.

Don't rule out loans insured by the FHA or partially guaranteed by the VA. Such loans carry fixed interest rates, significantly below regular rates—though you will have to pay points to the conventional lender. An FHA-insured loan can be a good bet if you're refinancing, too. Both types of loans are assumable. In a typical area, the limit on a loan insured by the FHA is around $70,000; the VA will currently guarantee $27,500 of a loan.

Once you have found a lender who offers a mortgage with attractive terms, your next step is to try to get some concessions. Your best bet is to speak with someone high up—for example, the vice president in charge of mortgages.

EXHIBIT 2-2

MONTHLY MORTGAGE PAYMENTS PER $1,000

Annual interest rate	20 years	25 years	30 years
8¼	$ 8.525	$ 7.892	$ 7.517
8½	8.683	8.058	7.692
8¾	8.842	8.225	7.875
9	9.000	8.400	8.050
9¼	9.167	8.567	8.233
9½	9.325	8.742	8.417
9¾	9.492	8.917	8.592
10	9.813	9.087	8.780
10½	9.990	9.450	9.150
10¾	10.160	9.630	9.340
11	10.322	9.801	9.523
11½	10.664	10.165	9.903
12	11.011	10.532	10.286
12½	11.361	10.904	10.673
13	11.716	11.278	11.062
13½	12.074	11.656	11.454
14	12.435	12.038	11.849
15	13.168	12.808	12.640
16	13.913	13.589	13.270
17	14.668	14.378	14.060

Example: You obtain a 20-year mortgage of $50,000 at 12 percent interest. Your monthly payment of both principal and interest will be $11.011 (from the table) times 50 (the units of one thousand in the loan), which equals $550.55.

"Too many people," says Dr. Fribush, "make the mistake of thinking that they can't bargain with a banker. They're awed by bankers. Don't be. Too much money is at stake."

THE PERILS OF CREATIVE FINANCING

Suppose you have moved heaven and earth, and you still can't get a big enough mortgage—or you can't find a buyer who can obtain a big enough mortgage. Well, welcome to the world of creative financing.

What virtually all forms of creative financing have in common is that the seller helps the buyer financially—he "takes back some paper." When mortgage money is scarce, sellers eager to unload make all sorts of financial arrangements with buyers. These deals are often perilous to the seller; sometimes they are perilous to the buyer.

A seller might lend the buyer all the money he needs, and get first dibs on the proceeds if the house has to be sold to pay the debt. That's a first mortgage, or a purchase-money mortgage. In a second mortgage, the seller has—naturally—second dibs on the house in a foreclosure sale. Let's say a buyer already has a $75,000 mortgage and a $50,000 down payment; you're selling the house for $200,000. You make up the $75,000 balance by means of a second mortgage.

For sellers, the obvious danger is that the buyer will default. You can lengthen the odds against a buyer's defaulting on a first mortgage by having your lawyer scrupulously examine his credit rating, employment record, assets, and so forth. If yours is a second mortgage, check with the first mortgagor. In either case, consider asking for a "certified financial statement" from the buyer's accountant. If the buyer is self-employed, look over his past tax returns to corroborate his income and assets. On a second mortgage, you might even insist upon the buyer's giving you extra collateral, like negotiable securities.

On a first mortgage, make sure you get a hefty down payment, so the buyer won't be tempted to walk away without paying off the balance of the loan. The down payment should be at least 30 percent of the house's selling price.

With a second mortgage, there's a danger that the buyer will default on only his first mortgage, the lender will foreclose, and you won't learn about it until after the foreclosure sale. So have the first lender tell you if the buyer defaults, by means of a "request for notice of default."

Any small second mortgage is risky. A buyer may know how long, costly ($10,000 is typical), and messy a foreclosure sale is. So a bad hat of a buyer might pay up on his first mortgage and stop paying your piddling second mortgage, trusting you'll be rational enough not to spend $10,000 or more trying to regain $5,000.

If you simply must give a buyer a first or second mortgage, you must get seller mortgage insurance. You can even get such insurance for a mortgage you gave a buyer a few years ago, and even on a second mortgage. But wonders do cease. If a buyer defaults because of a balloon mortgage, where the whole loan comes due at once after a few years, the insurance coverage won't cover your losses.

What losses? Sure, you can still sell the house again. But you might have extraordinarily high foreclosure costs. You might have to sell the house very quickly, at a terrible loss, because you need money to keep paying the mortgage on the new house you bought. Or you might not be able to sell the house for anywhere near the price you first got, because your buyer has let the house deteriorate something awful.

To obtain seller mortgage insurance, you must deal with a local lending institution—a savings and loan association, a commercial bank, a mortgage banker. The lending institution will run a credit check on the buyer, then have you and the buyer fill out standard mortgage forms. Later, the lending institution will "service" the loan—collect the monthly payments and perhaps put aside money into an escrow account for property taxes. Almost all lending institutions have arrangements to get mortgage insurance from companies like Mortgage Guaranty Insurance Corp. (MGIC) in Milwaukee or Verex Assurance in Madison, Wis. Such insurance covers whatever loss you may sustain simply because of foreclosure costs.

If you have already given a buyer a mortgage, the lending institution will check the forms to see if there are any loopholes. If you tight-fistedly wrote up the contract yourself, following your own mortgage contract, or if you used a lawyer unfamiliar with real estate, you may be out of luck. But there's still a chance. You can have an experienced lawyer draw up new papers for you and the buyer to sign. The lending institution, and then the mortgage insurer, may approve.

There will be two charges: for the lending institution's work and for the insurance itself. Some lending institutions levy a one-time charge of 1 to 2 percent of the total loan, plus a yearly fee (like $120) for servicing the loan. MGIC typically charges ½ percent of the total loan during the first year, and .25 percent every year after that. Sellers' mortgages usually run five to 10 years.

How much coverage should you get? On a first mortgage, you need only 20 percent of the loan insured. That should cover all you might lose in a hasty foreclosure sale. On a second mortgage, you will need a lot more. While 100 percent coverage is available, 80 percent should do nicely.

If you are just applying for mortgage insurance, you can expect the buyer to pay the lending institution's charges and for the cost of the insurance itself. But if the mortgage is already in effect, you'll probably have to pay all the freight.

Later on, if you need cash, you may be able to sell your mortgage, at a discount, to the Federal National Mortgage Association or some other company. Fannie Mae, however, will not buy a mortgage that exceeds $107,000.

Besides obtaining insurance if you give a buyer a mortgage, make sure the contract has a due-on-sale clause, so the buyer cannot (in most states) sell the house along with the mortgage to someone unreliable. And be sure that the buyer has adequate home insurance, payable to you in case of a claim on the house. Insist on seeing the policy.

Whatever kind of mortgage you provide a buyer with, naturally, don't make it a long-term, fixed-rate mortgage at a very moderate interest rate.

Much more sensible for the seller is a *balloon mortgage*. The buyer pays the seller for, say, five years, at a moderate rate of interest, as if the loan were really due in 25 or 30 years. Then the balloon pops, and the whole shmeer comes due. At this point, the buyer—it is to be hoped—can get reasonable terms from traditional lenders. In reality, buyers, once their balloons have burst, have *not* always been able to get reasonable outside financing. The best course for the seller, in these circumstances, is to go ahead and renew the mortgage, perhaps with another balloon after three to five years. That is, unless he wants to be hard-hearted and foreclose. (Foreclosures caused by balloon mortgages, remember, are *not* covered by mortgage insurance.)

There are other ways to make it easier for buyers to repay a purchase-money mortgage. For example, have them pay only the interest on the loan during the first few years, not the principal. (If a second mortgage is involved, and there are no payments at all for a while, it's called a *sleeping second*.)

Very much different from the second mortgage and the purchase-money mortgage is the *installment contract*. The buyer gets a loan from the seller, but doesn't receive title to the house until the loan is mostly paid off—usually 60 percent of it. This protects the seller to a degree. He doesn't have to foreclose if the buyer defaults early on, and he gets to keep his house. But should the buyer be a nerd, he may neglect to pay the property taxes and let the house itself fall apart. If he defaults, whatever he has paid you may not be enough to satisfy overdue taxes and restore your property. And if there was an enforceable due-on-sale clause in the seller's contract, everyone is in Dutch.

Then there's the *lease-option*. The prospective buyer lives in your house and pays you a rent high enough to cover your mortgage payments. Meanwhile, he has an option to buy your house once mortgage money becomes available. You can let part or all of the rent go towards the purchase of the house—the price of which generally stays the same. One catch here is that if you give someone a lease with an option to buy, you may run afoul of your lender's due-on-sale clause.

Still another possibility—is there no end?—is the *ground lease*. The buyer purchases the house but rents the ground underneath. This means he can make a smaller down payment and smaller mortgage payments—the land may be 25 percent of the purchase price. In a few years, the buyer may have saved enough money to buy the land, too. But this is a tricky business. The buyer in a ground lease may not be eligible for the postponement of capital-gains taxes when he sells, or for the one-time $125,000 capital-gains exclusion. (See Chapter 6.)

And now we come to three devices that should be rather attractive to both buyers and sellers.

First: the *wraparound mortgage*. The seller continues to pay his old low-interest mortgage, without (sometimes) telling the lender that his house has been sold. The buyer ends up with one mortgage, a combination of the seller's old low-interest mortgage and a second mortgage at a higher rate. Together, they give him a mortgage at a moderate rate. The main thing wrong with a wraparound is that, if there's a due-on-sale clause in the original mortgage, it may be illegal.

Second: the *blend mortgage*. The seller or buyer visits the lender of the original mortgage and asks whether he is really eager to get the seller's chintzy old low-interest-rate mortgage off the books. If so, the lender may be willing to grant the buyer a mortgage with a moderate interest rate. The new rate is a blend of the old mortgage rate and the current market rate. (Confusingly, wraparounds arranged by lenders themselves are sometimes called blend mortgages.)

Third: the *buy-down*. The seller gives the lender some cash, which the lender uses to provide the buyer with a mortgage that, during the first few years, carries a low interest rate. Three years is typical. A few thousand dollars could knock down an interest rate several percentage points. And it's a one-time charge. Consider, too, that reducing the price of a house to lower the buyer's mortgage rate that much would cost the seller vastly more money—because of the longer term involved, 20 years (say) as against three. These days, many builders are offering buy-downs on new houses.

Which creative-financing device is best for both buyer and seller is hard to say. So much depends on whether the seller needs cash to buy a new house, whether or not the original mortgage has an enforceable due-on-sale clause, whether the seller can get private mortgage insurance on his loan to the buyer, how merciful and generous the seller is, how reliable and trustworthy the buyer. The place to start, probably, is with a blend mortgage. After that, consult your broker, your accountant, your lawyer, and various lenders. Large amounts of money are at stake. Don't go it alone.

To make matters even more complicated, there are obvious alternatives for sellers thinking of creative financing.

• Consider dropping the price of your house. After all, that's what you're doing, indirectly, when you offer a buyer a mortgage at a moderate interest rate. And with a lower price, you will owe your broker a smaller commission.

• Consider renting—temporarily—until interest rates drop, and buyers with their own mortgages happen along.

As for poor Dr. Lee, whom we left scrounging around for a mortgage to buy a condominium, his father rode to his rescue by lending him enough to buy the condominium outright.

That's an alternative that buyers should consider.

CHAPTER 3

DIRTY TRICKS SOME BROKERS PLAY

Several years ago, Mr. and Mrs. John Carter (not their real name) of upstate New York bought a house they did not like. And as Mrs. Carter recalls, it wasn't the devil but their saleswoman who made them do it.

"We were really set up," says Mrs. Carter. "The agent showed us quite a few shabby houses first. They were in the $60,000s and $70,000s, and they looked as if they had just been cleaned up to pass a board of health minimum inspection. We got the impression that the only homes we could afford were like that. So when the broker showed us a new Tudor house, by comparison it looked wonderful, and we bought it. It was actually clean!

"There was another house we were interested in. It was elegantly decorated, had cathedral ceilings, a wet bar. But the agent kept telling us it was too expensive. She had the listing on the Tudor, not on the other house. Now, every time we drive past that other house we didn't buy, we feel heartsick.

"We bought the Tudor at full price. The agent told us that *all* new houses sell for full price. Later, a house near ours, almost identical to ours and built by the same builder, was reduced by $5,000. And the agent didn't keep her promises. She told us that the seller would pay $400 for new wallpaper, $700 for shrubbery. Why didn't we put all that into the contract? Well, agents ingratiate themselves with you.

When they pat you on the back, keep buying coffee for you and treating you at McDonald's, you build up a friendly relationship. You stop being business-minded."

The Carters, who are both in their 30s, have learned their lesson. They put their Tudor up for sale and are looking again for a house they really like. "But now we don't believe anything agents say," declares Mrs. Carter.

The majority of real-estate brokers and salesmen are honest and conscientious. They take pride in the valuable services they perform: (1) helping sellers set reasonable prices on their property, make their houses more salable, and find qualified buyers; and (2) helping buyers obtain homes and mortgages appropriate to their needs, tastes, and wallets.

Still, the Carters' sour experience was not unique. They simply fell for some old tricks, including one recommended in a textbook for real-estate agents, *California Real Estate Practice* by Robert J. Bond:* "In the sequence of showing, it is usually best to start with the least probable choice first, and finish with the most likely.... By so doing, the probable selection is better appreciated because of the more favorable appearance when compared to those previously shown."

There are out-and-out crooks among real-estate agents, of course. A classic case in point: A man in Florida wanted to buy a house; the asking price, an agent told him, was $75,000. The man made a down payment. When he finally received the legal papers, he learned that he had purchased the house from the agent. The agent had used the man's down payment to purchase the house himself, at a cost of $37,500, and proceeded to sell it for $75,000.

Agents have sold houses without telling buyers that the heating system wasn't working, that the place was infested with termites, or that the property was much smaller than originally described. In one memorable case, an agent managed to sell a building without letting the buyer know that it had recently been condemned.

Other agents have persuaded sellers to raise the price of their property by adding on another bedroom, enclosing a porch, and so on, and later quietly pocketed kickbacks from the contractors.

But the out-and-out crooks among real-estate agents are rare. The ones to really worry about, because they are more common, are the money-minded manipulators.

---

* Excerpts reprinted courtesy of Robert J. Bond, Realtor, Ph.D.

Books for real-estate people advocate prevarication, intimidation, dissembling—anything for a buck. Jack I. Pyle, a broker in Maitland, Fla., claims that in 19 years in real estate he has found that "too few brokers are more interested in the client than in the commission he represents." Capturing an attitude prevalent in the real-estate world is the advice given by a broker in the magazine *Real Estate Today* (published by the National Association of Realtors): "I tell my salesmen that when someone walks through the front door, they should picture him with a $1,000 bill taped to his forehead." (The broker modifies this advice by adding that you can win the $1,000 by listening to and caring for the customer.)

The following list of dirty tricks played on buyers and sellers has been obtained from state real-estate commissions, from books about real-estate sales, and from brokers and salesmen themselves. Just knowing that a particular trick exists should help protect you from being victimized.

"ALL SELLERS ARE STORYTELLERS"
What an agent wants from the seller, first of all, is the exclusive right to sell his house. Let's say that you advertise that your house is "For Sale by Owner." According to Joan Haberle, former secretary-director of the New Jersey Real Estate Commission, an agent may drive up to your home, introduce himself, and tell you that he has a couple outside in the car who have fallen madly in love with your home. But they are adamant that he act as the agent. You peek outside; the attractive young couple inside the car wave and smile. Just so they will look at your house, you sign an exclusive contract with the agent. As it turns out, the couple like your house but don't buy. Actually, they're salespeople employed by the broker.

Agents have other ways of manipulating you if you try to sell your house yourself. They may telephone you, without identifying themselves as agents, get the information they need, and make an appointment to see the house. Once they have taken up a lot of your time, they finally announce that they are really agents.

After the real-estate agent has signed you up, his next goal may be to get you to underprice your house. True, the higher the price, the higher his commission, but unprofessional agents want quick sales. The difference between a 6 percent commission on a $200,000 house and on a $180,000 house is $1,200. But it may take three months to sell a house at $200,000, a weekend to sell it at $180,000. In fact, if a broker wants to get rich selling residential real estate, he should sell lots and lots of underpriced properties. One very successful broker admits that he handles only houses priced at, or below, their real value.

Even if a seller insists on putting a fair or somewhat inflated price on his property, agents can knock it down. There's a saying in real estate: "All sellers are storytellers." Under the proper pressure, even sellers who swear that they will never budge will budge.

One powerful tactic is for the agent to just let the seller's house sit. And sit. As Robert Irwin writes in his book *Protect Yourself in Real Estate,** "The broker knows that as time goes by without a sale, you will get more desperate." So he just ignores your listing. "No buyers come by to see the house for weeks or even months," Irwin writes. "When you check the papers, you discover that your home is almost never advertised. Or when you call the agent's office pretending to be a buyer looking for a house just like yours, you are told by a salesman that no such home is on the market, but others are available." Eventually, "you may find yourself accepting a lower price and less advantageous terms than you normally would."

Other agents will put psychological pressure on the seller to accept a low offer. When one agent gets such an offer, he rushes to the seller and enthusiastically tells him the wonderful news that his house has been sold. Later, he slips in the bad news—the wretchedly low offer.

Similarly, a broker quoted in *Real Estate Today* says: "We spend a lot of time enthusiastically acting as if we had sold the home while explaining all we did to get there. The salesman tries to convey his own excitement about an imminent sale to the seller. Many times the drama does a lot to make the offer look a lot better than if the salesman had just laid it out cold in the first place."

Even before rushing over to the seller with the joyous news that there's a miserably low offer on his house, the agent may have softened him up already. He may have persuaded him to buy another house—without putting a clause in the purchase agreement giving him time to sell the first one. That way, the seller will be anxious, and likely to accept an offer below his asking price.

---

* Excerpts reprinted from *Protect Yourself in Real Estate* by Robert Irwin. Copyright © 1977 by McGraw-Hill Book Company. Used with the permission of McGraw-Hill Book Company.

DIRTY TRICKS SOME BROKERS PLAY

If sellers are not cooperative, brokers may bring in the heavy artillery. Robert Irwin knows a broker whose listing on a house was about to expire. So she induced a buyer to offer $7,000 less than the asking price. Naturally, the seller—a divorcée—refused it. A few days later, the broker had her brother and sister-in-law make an offer on the house—$10,000 below the asking price. The seller, shaken, again refused. But she had been set up for the kill. When the broker had the first bidder offer $7,000 less again, the seller, bewildered and frightened, accepted.

Agents who induce sellers to underprice their houses may have other motives besides wanting quick commissions. One broker talked a seller into accepting a low offer, and it was only later that the seller learned that the buyer was the broker's father-in-law. (That broker lost his license.)

Finally, don't assume that all brokers will automatically bring you the highest offers they receive. Suppose the listing broker has two offers on your house. One is from a buyer he found; one is from a buyer associated with another broker. (This broker would be entitled to part of the commission if that buyer got the house.) In order to collect a full commission and not just part, the listing broker may tell you about only the offer from his own buyer—even if the other offer was higher.

Joan Haberle reports this variation: Your broker gets three bids on your house. One is for $196,000, but the buyer wants to move in within three months. One is for $195,000, subject to the buyer's being able to get a low-interest mortgage. The third is for $193,000 cash. "Which is the broker likely to bring to you?" Haberle asks. "Right. The third one. Because there's less work for the broker that way."

To protect yourself against such tactics, here are some rules to follow:

1. Insist that an agent apprise you of all offers he receives on your house, not just the ones he cares to tell you about.

2. If an agent ever offers, as a great favor, to buy your house himself ("It's my fault it hasn't sold—I overpriced it"), consider the possibility that your house is *under*priced.

3. If an agent importunes you to reduce the price of your house just before his listing expires, resist. A new broker may work harder to sell your house, and may be able to get you your full price.

4. Never tell an agent that you are under pressure to sell your house. He may interpret this to mean that you are amenable to ridiculously low offers.

"ALL BUYERS ARE LIARS"

From buyers, unprofessional agents want just what they want from sellers—fast action and quick commissions. Here is how they go about getting them:

First, of course, by obtaining your name and phone number, and—even better—getting you into their office.

Let's say that you see an ad for a real creampuff: an underpriced house in a desirable neighborhood. You call the agency, and a salesman urges you to hurry in. When you arrive, the creampuff has turned into a vanishing creampuff. It has just been sold. But as long as you're here, the salesman oilily suggests, why don't you hop into his car and let him show you another house almost as wonderful?

There are various explanations for what happened. Perhaps the salesman deliberately misled you. This advice for real-estate agents comes from Robert Bond's book: "Often the ad about which the prospect is calling is still running, although the property is sold. The salesman might say, 'We just got the listings. Come right on in. It's a real hot deal.' When they arrive, you say, 'I'm sorry, the house was just sold, but we have another that probably has just what you're looking for. Let's hurry and get in right away. It may not last.' "

Or perhaps the house was never really for sale—the ad is bait to lure customers in. Lawyer Kenneth S. Gaines of Van Nuys, Calif., reports in his book *How to Sell (and Buy) Your Home* that "a broker friend of mine advertises such a house and he owns it himself. If he were ever to sell it, he would have to change his entire advertising campaign."

The house may not even exist. A New Jersey broker says that he occasionally sees an ad for a house that he doesn't recognize. Since he and the listing broker belong to the same multiple-listing system, he telephones. "They're evasive," he says. "They're not sure which house it is. Or they tell me it might be such-and-such a house—and the only relation between *that* house and the one advertised is the price."

Once an agent has gotten you into his office, he sets about gaining your trust. To win customers over, Robert Bond urges, "convince them that you really care for them, that you are concerned about their needs, and that you regard them as important." One broker tells buyers that his job is to help them, not to sell them.

What's wrong with that? Well, by contrast, here is what one former broker—Jeanne Hannafin, now deputy administrator of the Nevada State Real Estate Commission—used to tell *her* customers: "Although I'll try to be fair, my primary concern and obligation is to the seller. He pays my commission. If at any point you feel you need representation, you should consider hiring a lawyer."

In fact, Benny L. Kass, a real-estate lawyer in Washington, D.C., believes that the single biggest offense that real-estate agents are guilty of is pretending to be the allies of the buyers when they are legally the agents of the sellers.

The first thing you may want to tell your new friend the agent is how much money you can comfortably spend on a house. The agent, on the other hand, may want to know how much you can *really* spend on a house, comfortably or uncomfortably. All buyers, as agents say, are liars.

An agent may "test" a buyer's price. One agent writes that, after the buyer has given his "absolute limit," he will quickly change the subject. Then, sometime later, he begins describing a luxurious house that has everything the buyer wants—and more. But the price is considerably above the buyer's limit. When the buyer hesitates, then decides to look the place over, he has lost.

Next, an agent will start showing you houses for sale. Unprofessional agents never show anyone more than three to five houses—even though the buyer may be a transferee unfamiliar with the area and local prices, or a novice unfamiliar with different types of houses. Unprofessional agents will also show you houses only within a circumscribed area. Robert Irwin asks this question: "If one area has a dozen houses for which you might easily qualify, while another has only one, which you could just barely afford, which area do you think the broker will suggest?" His advice: "Insist on seeing homes in the area that is just above your reach."

Before actually taking you to see houses, unprofessional agents may have warned sellers to conceal any defects in their homes. Many brokers, in fact, don't think it's their job to let buyers know what defects a house has. A 1976 poll of Realtors* in Denver, Dallas, and Kansas City found that most agreed

---
* A Realtor is a broker who belongs to the National Association of Realtors. A salesman works for a broker. Real-estate agents are either brokers or salesmen.

with this statement: "In the purchase of a home, it is the buyer's responsibility to detect any malfunctions or defects in the home." Many states' real-estate commissions, however, require agents to reveal to buyers any defects they know about. And many courts have held that if agents conceal any defects, they are liable.

The best time to show houses, some agents believe, is sunset. "The mood is more reflective, if not more romantic," writes Bond, "and the setting more beautiful." John Sakson, a lawyer formerly with the New Jersey Real Estate Commission, adds that at night prospective buyers may not notice the supermarket only two houses away, the watermarks in the basement, or the lime sprinkled over the spot in the yard where the septic tank erupted.

And if any buyers should perversely concern themselves with such petty details, agents may be prepared with ready answers to their objections. Bond gives this conversation as an example:

"My, what a dirty house!"
"Yes, but look at the price."
"There's no dining room."
"One less room for your wife to clean."

A tried-and-true method to get a buyer who is wavering to commit himself is to talk about all the other buyers who are supposedly interested in the house, all set to pounce. "If you listen to brokers," says Benny Kass, "the entire Red Chinese army is ready to buy that home you're looking at."

Obviously, what buyers need when they are considering houses, more than anything else, is time. Time to compare, time to ponder. But time is the one thing that many agents refuse to give them.

A recent issue of *Real Estate Today* carries the article "How Not to Take 'NO' for an Answer." In it, the author warns fellow agents that if potential buyers are allowed to go home after seeing several houses for sale, their ardor may cool. "So," he goes on, "what is needed is a method to get the buyers into the office. During the showing process, the buyers usually ask technical questions about the square footage, taxes, school district, insulation, and so on. Instead of rattling off an answer, say, 'I don't have that information with me, but when we get back to the office, I will look it up for you.' . . . Now you are able to get them into the office and into a closing situation."

To protect yourself against these and other pitfalls:

1. Don't stick with one broker. If you use more than one, and they know they have competition, they may whisk you off to see desirable houses just as soon as they come on the market. And if you tell one agent that you're thinking of buying a house another agent showed you, the first may treat you to a useful catalogue of everything wrong with that house and that neighborhood.

2. If an agent begins browbeating you to buy a house, remember: Just because you lose an argument doesn't mean you have to buy a house. If you're arguing and logic fails you, fall back on illogic. Say that you don't want a particular house because it reminds you of your mother-in-law.

3. Don't relax your defenses with an agent, the way Mr. and Mrs. Carter did, even if he says he wants to help you. One broker, in print, has even urged his colleagues to sell a house "you personally think is a dog."

CHAPTER 4

HOW TO HAGGLE FOR FUN AND PROFIT

The architect who had designed the house had lived there—always a good sign. It featured floor-to-ceiling windows, a gargantuan fireplace, two kitchens, two patios, closets everywhere. At $72,900, it was a steal. I saw it the very first day it came on the market, but as I was not familiar with the community, I needed a few hours to do research. When I returned with my bid of $69,000, the house had already been sold—for exactly $72,900.

Lessons I learned: (1) If you are very much taken with a house that has just come on the market, put a binder on it immediately. (2) If you are lucky enough to find a genuine bargain, don't bother to bargain.

Actually, if the house had been for sale for two or three months without selling and without a recent price cut, a low bid would have been appropriate. But sellers are rightly loath to accept low bids on houses just offered for sale—why throw in the towel so soon?—and most buyers know it. Hence the truth in the truism, "The first offer is the best offer."

BARGAINING RULES
The first thing to find out about any house you are interested in buying is how long it has been for sale. The agent or seller should tell you. With a newly listed house, or one whose price has recently been slashed, you have little

leeway to bargain. But with a house that has limped along for months and months, you can haggle to your heart's content.

Another thing to determine before the bargaining begins is a price you think reasonable for the house, a price you can afford. It may be easier for you to decide upon the figure at which the house would be decidedly overpriced and that would warrant your looking elsewhere.

Also figure out beforehand what you can bargain with besides money. A buyer, after all, could offer to shift the moving-in day according to the seller's wishes. The seller could offer to throw those handsome brass fireplace andirons into the kitty, shift his own moving day, or—if he is giving the buyer a mortgage—stretch out the term a bit.

The buyer's or seller's spouse should be tactfully instructed to keep quiet during the bargaining. Someone who doesn't know the rules can louse everything up. I once witnessed the following colloquy:

Seller: $200,000, and that's my final offer!
Buyer: I don't see how I can possibly afford that.
Buyer's wife: (Groans.)

The seller, of course, got the message: The wife was in love with the house. By the same token, a seller's spouse who has to be repeatedly shushed during the bargaining is conveying the message that he or she thinks the seller should give in.

Buyers should also be wary of agents. The agent, remember, is legally on the seller's side. If you tell the agent that you will offer $170,000 for a house priced at $200,000, but go as high as $180,000, a good agent will tell the seller what you are up to. Good agents have told me as much. You would never get the house for less than $180,000, and you might have to pay more. Neither buyer nor seller should tell the agent that he is under any pressure—the buyer, say, to move out of his old house, the seller to move into his new one. During the bargaining session, the agent may take the side of the party who is not subject to any time pressures, thinking that the deal can be wrapped up faster that way.

Neither buyer nor seller should make himself obnoxious. Sellers, furious at certain unlovable buyers, have been known to sell their houses to other buyers for less money. Buyers have walked away from houses they wanted simply because the sellers proved so nasty. And a clumsy, unskillful bargainer can easily make himself obnoxious. A buyer should therefore go easy on criticizing a house in front of the seller. You could emphasize instead that you admire the house, but that you just don't have the money that the seller is hardheartedly demanding. Plead poverty. Poor-mouth at every turn. If you do denigrate a house, do it with circumspection. Don't belittle the seller's taste—the frightful wallpaper, for example. Mention the water stains in the attic, the high heating bills, the noisy sump pump in the basement, the limited closet space.

Of course, it will do no good for the buyer to plead poverty if he is known to be well-off. Doctors should not announce to the world that they are doctors when they go house-hunting. The seller should also poor-mouth it. He is trying to buy another home, for $300,000, and needs every penny from the sale of his current house. Experiments have shown that when people bargain for new cars, they get the best prices if they are dressed shabbily. It underscores their poverty.

Before bargaining, you should know how to deal with the killers. These are statements like "This is my final offer" and "Take it or leave it." The best response is simply to ignore them and keep bargaining. As for that other killer, "Let's split the difference," just say, "I'd love to, but I can't afford it."

THE MAIN EVENT
Since sellers typically overprice a house by 5 to 10 percent, the shrewd buyer's first bid should normally be about 15 percent below the asking price. Unless, of course, the buyer thinks the house is priced even *more* than 10 percent above what it is really worth. So as not to plunge the seller into a state of shock, be timid about the first, low bid. If a house is priced at $200,000 and you might want it for $180,000, offer $170,000—but timidly, explaining to the agent or the seller that even that figure is stretching your budget.

Then pray that the seller makes a counter-offer. Experiments have proved that the bargainer who makes the most rapid concessions, and makes them first, usually winds up paying too much or getting too little.

The buyer's subsequent concessions (and the seller's) should be slow, reluctant, painful, piteous. And they should follow a pattern. They should go from somewhat sizable concessions to minuscule concessions, and they should end up close to a nice, round, fat number—like $180,000. If a buyer starts the bidding with $170,000, he might later bid $173,000,

$175,000, $176,500, and $177,500. Those are increases of $3,000, $2,000, $1,500, and $1,000. The point of the decreasing concessions, of course, is to lower the other bargainer's expectations. The point of aiming toward a nice, round number is that it will seem like a fitting resting-place.

The entire bargaining period may take a few weeks. And at some point, the bargainers may hit an impasse. No one is willing to make the next concession.

One tactic at this point is to invoke the old killer, "My last offer was my final offer—I can't afford to budge." If that doesn't work, suggest a break—a cooling-off period. Often that will resolve an impasse. Or get away from money. The seller will throw in the garden furniture, for example.

There are two other splendid ways out of an impasse. One is for the buyer and the seller to gang up on the agent, browbeating him to lower the commission. If the impasse seems unbridgeable—and it is amazing, the degree to which egos can get involved—the agent may comply.

Then there is the tactic employed by an agent for Previews, a company in Greenwich, Conn., that sells unusual houses.

In 1947, Gerard B. Lambert, of the pharmaceutical company, told Previews that he wanted to sell his 500-acre Virginia estate for $275,000. The same day, Previews found a wealthy coal-mine owner who was willing to pay that price. The deal had almost gone through when a hitch developed. The buyer wanted to pay $25,000 extra for a Gilbert Stuart portrait of George Washington that hung in the foyer. Lambert was unwilling to part with it. The Previews agent suggested they toss a coin. They did. The buyer won. Impasse resolved.

DIRTY TRICKS DEPARTMENT
One joker to watch out for when bargaining is the "low-ball." It happened to a friend of mine. She was selling her house, and a buyer agreed to meet her price. A few weeks after signing a binder for a mere $50, the buyer announced that he had changed his mind. He was reducing his offer by $15,000. My friend stuck to her guns, swallowed her disappointment, and would not sell to him for a nickel less than the earlier price. The deal was off.

Phony offers are not uncommon in real estate. To guard against them, the seller should demand a large, nonrefundable deposit. And he should not throw away the names of competing buyers until the deal is closed. If the *seller* reneges, by the way, after a binder has been signed, the buyer can threaten to go to court and will have a good case.

What if you absolutely loathe the idea of bargaining? Some people do. You should then announce the fact—"I hate to bargain, and $190,000 is my final offer." Or say "I am offering a rock-bottom price because I want to sell fast."

The trouble is, if a buyer immediately offers $190,000 for a $200,000 house, the seller may greedily imagine he can eventually get $195,000. And if a seller offers a house at $200,000 "firm," many buyers will nonetheless believe they can knock a few thousand off the price. In other words, don't bargain if you don't want to. But expect trouble. Not being willing to bargain isn't exactly un-American, but it is untraditional.

CHAPTER

5 SURPRISING FACTS ABOUT HOMEOWNERS INSURANCE

Despite all the propaganda you hear, if you live in a pricey neighborhood, chances are that your house is *not* underinsured. In fact, in the view of Norman Hoffman, an assistant professor at The College of Insurance in New York, most homes are adequately insured. Those who think otherwise are confusing market value with replacement value. A house in Beverly Hills might sell for $250,000, but cost only $100,000 to rebuild if it burned down. The same holds true for houses in many other parts of the country where the market value exceeds the replacement value.

Support for Professor Hoffman comes from a survey of homeowners by Equifax Services, which provides property-inspection reports to the insurance industry. Equifax found that 58 percent of American homes are underinsured. But by "underinsured," Equifax meant anything less than *100* percent insured. As I'll explain below, a house that's insured for only *80* percent of its value isn't exactly "underinsured." So, overall, it would seem that well *over* 42 percent of American homes are adequately insured.

FROM HO 1 TO HO 8
Generally, homeowners insurance comes in packages. In one swoop, you get protection on

your house, its contents, and any detached buildings from all sorts of dangers. You also get liability insurance—protection against being financially responsible because you or a family member accidentally injures somebody or destroys somebody's property.

Homeowners policies come in varieties prefixed by the initials "HO," for homeowners. HO 1, according to Hoffman, is "limited and terrible." HO 5 is luxury coverage. HO 4 is for renters, HO 6 for condominium owners, HO 8 for owners of old gingerbread houses. HO 2 is not as good as HO 3, and HO 3 is what Hoffman and most other authorities recommend. It's neither luxurious nor stingy. Exhibit 5-1 shows what the various policies cover.

EXHIBIT 5-1

COMPARISON OF HOMEOWNERS INSURANCE POLICIES

Type of policy				Causes of loss
HO 1 (Basic)	HO 2 (Broad)	HO 3 (Special)	HO 5 (Comprehensive)	
X O	X O	X O	X O	Fire or lightning
X O	X O	X O	X O	Loss of property, not on premises, from fire or other perils
X O	X O	X O	X O	Windstorm or hail
X O	X O	X O	X O	Explosion
X O	X O	X O	X O	Riot or civil commotion
X O	X O	X O	X O	Aircraft, vehicles
X O	X O	X O	X O	Smoke
X O	X O	X O	X O	Vandalism and malicious mischief
X O	X O	X O	X O	Theft
X O	X O	X	X O	Breakage of glass constituting part of the building
	X O	X O	X O	Falling objects
	X O	X O	X O	Weight of ice, snow

Source: Insurance Information Institute.

SURPRISING FACTS ABOUT HOMEOWNERS INSURANCE

	Type of policy			Causes of loss
HO 1 (Basic)	HO 2 (Broad)	HO 3 (Special)	HO 5 (Comprehensive)	
	X O	X O	X O	Collapse of building or any part
	X O	X O	X O	Sudden and accidental tearing apart, cracking, burning, or bulging of a steam or hot-water heating system or of appliances for heating water
	X O	X O	X O	Accidental discharge, leakage, or overflow of water or steam from within a plumbing, heating, or air-conditioning system or domestic appliance
	X O	X O	X O	Freezing of plumbing, heating, or air-conditioning equipment and domestic appliances
	X O	X O	X O	Sudden and accidental injury from artificially generated currents to electrical appliances, devices, fixtures, and wiring (TV and radio tubes not included)
			X O	All perils except flood, earthquake, war, nuclear accident, and others mentioned in your policy

X = Dwelling
O = Contents

You get a bargain if you insure your house for only 80 percent of its replacement value. You will be compensated 100 percent if there is only partial damage to your residence. If 50 percent of your house is destroyed, for instance, you will be compensated for that 50 percent. But if it's a total loss, you will get only 80 percent of the replacement value. With the high cost of houses these days, you might be wise to insure your house for 90 or 100 percent of its replacement value.

If your $200,000 house is insured for 80 percent of its replacement value ($160,000), you automatically get half that coverage on the personal property in your house: $80,000. You are also entitled to 10 percent of the insurance on the dwelling for coverage of garages, tool sheds, gazebos, and other detached buildings. This would be $16,000. And you are entitled to 20 percent of the total for living costs if your house is uninhabitable—up to $32,000 for (1) temporary living quarters and (2) the difference between what meals would have cost at home and what they cost out.

FLOATERS AND RIDERS
There are limits, alas, on coverage for expensive individual items you own, such as furs, jewelry, silverware, and watches. Sit down with your agent or broker and get "floaters" on those items, covering them for full or nearly full value if they are destroyed or stolen. Expect to pay $1 to $2.75 for $100 of jewelry coverage and $1 for $100 of furs. (An *agent,* by the way, works for insurance companies, a *broker* works for *you.*)

As for the ordinary personal property you own, if it's destroyed or stolen you will receive only the depreciated value. So you should get a "replacement cost" rider. This guarantees that if your ratty old sofa is destroyed, you will be paid not for the value of a ratty old sofa, but for a spanking new one. "You get new for old," says Hoffman.

You should also get "valued" policy coverage on the contents of your home, so that there isn't any argument over the value of something destroyed or missing. And you should boot out any nasty "pair and set" clause in your policy, so that if one earring vanishes or one painting from a triptych by da Vinci is ruined, you are paid for the loss of the whole set, not just for the one item.

Homeowners policies also provide protection against medical expenses for which you are responsible—$25,000 per acci-

SURPRISING FACTS ABOUT HOMEOWNERS INSURANCE

dent, $500 per person. You need more. "And these days," says Hoffman, "no one knows how much is enough." Try $1 million. You can add that coverage, and more, to your homeowners policy by buying a "personal umbrella" policy. Such coverage is sometimes called, for good reason, sleep insurance. Cost: at least $125 a year.

Ask your agent or broker whether your area qualifies for flood insurance, or call 800-424-8872. The Federal Insurance Administration of the U.S. Department of Housing and Urban Development makes flood insurance available in flood-prone areas for low cost. But your property must be in a community that has agreed to plan and carry out measures to reduce future flooding. Such insurance is available in about 17,000 American communities.

Earthquake insurance is sold mainly to Californians. People living on the Pacific Coast should inquire about it.

If you employ someone on your premises—a gardener, a baby-sitter—ask your agent or broker to explain how workers' compensation insurance laws apply in your state and how they affect your liability if any employee is injured.

TAKING INVENTORY

Stop procrastinating and make a list of your major household belongings. Use the forms in Exhibit 5-2. Write down the purchase prices and the purchase dates, and attach receipts if possible. Photograph each wall of each room of your house with the closets and cabinet doors open. On the back of each photo, write the date, location, and the contents pictured. Keep the originals of your photos, as well as your inventory, in a safe-deposit box. Keep negatives of the photos (or duplicates) at home, along with a copy of the inventory, to remind you to update them every once in a while. The lazy way: Carry a tape recorder with you as you walk around the house describing your major possessions.

SAVING ON HOMEOWNERS INSURANCE

Shop around when you are looking for a policy. Get quotations from three different companies. Charges may vary considerably. When one homeowner in Selleville, Ill., was getting $50,000 worth of insurance on his home, quotations ranged from $168 a year to $244.

Continued on page 53

EXHIBIT 5-2

HOUSEHOLD INVENTORY

LIVING ROOM

Article & description	Purchase date	Purchase price
Carpet/rugs		
Curtains/drapes		
Sofas		
Chairs		
Coffee tables		
End tables		
Tables		
Desk		
Wall hangings		
Clocks		
Lamps		
Television		
Radio/stereo		
Records/tapes		
Books		
Musical instruments		
Plants/planters		
Mirrors		
Accessories		

Source: Insurance Information Institute.

SURPRISING FACTS ABOUT HOMEOWNERS INSURANCE

Article & description	Purchase date	Purchase price
Other		
Total		

PORCH/PATIO

Article & description	Purchase date	Purchase price
Chairs		
Tables		
Umbrella		
Floor covering		
Lamps		
Outdoor cooking equipment		
Plants/planters		
Other		
Total		

EXHIBIT 5-2 (Cont'd)

HOUSEHOLD INVENTORY

BEDROOMS

Article & description	Purchase date	Purchase price
Bookcases		
Chairs		
Carpet/rugs		
Curtains/drapes		
Beds		
Mattresses		
Cedar chest		
Desk		
Dressers		
Dressing tables		
Night tables		
Lamps		
Mirrors		
Clocks		
Radios		
Sewing machine		
Television		
Toilet articles		
Wall hangings		
Clothing		

Article & description	Purchase date	Purchase price
Other		
Total		

GARAGE/BASEMENT/ATTIC

Article & description	Purchase date	Purchase price
Furniture		
Luggage/trunks		
Sports equipment		
Toys		
Outdoor games		
Ornamental lawn items		
Lawn mower		
Shovels		
Spreaders		
Sprinklers/hoses		
Wheelbarrow		
Snow blower		
Garden tools/supplies		
Ladders/stepstools		
Workbench		

EXHIBIT 5-2 (Cont'd)

HOUSEHOLD INVENTORY

GARAGE/BASEMENT/ATTIC (Cont'd)

Article & description	Purchase date	Purchase price
Carpentry tools/supplies		
Canned goods/supplies		
Pet supplies		
Other		
Total		

KITCHEN

Article & description	Purchase date	Purchase price
Tables		
Chairs		
Curtains		
Cabinets		
Lighting fixtures		
Bowls		
Pots/pans		
Utensils		
Cutlery		
Dishes		

Article & description	Purchase date	Purchase price
Refrigerator		
Stove		
Dishwasher		
Disposal unit		
Freezer		
Washer		
Dryer		
Small appliances		
Clocks		
Radios		
Stepstool		
Food/supplies		
Other		
Total		

DINING ROOM

Article & description	Purchase date	Purchase price
Carpet/rugs		
Curtains/drapes		
Buffet		
Tables		
Chairs		

EXHIBIT 5-2 (Cont'd)

HOUSEHOLD INVENTORY

DINING ROOM (Cont'd)

Article & description	Purchase date	Purchase price
China cabinet		
China		
Silverware		
Glassware		
Clocks		
Lamps/fixtures		
Wall hangings		
Serving table/cart		
Other		
Total		

BATHROOM

Clothes hamper		
Curtains		
Dressing table		
Electrical appliances		
Scale		
Shower curtains		
Linens		
Other		
Total		

Consider a big $500 deductible, if you can get it, so that your premium is lower—unless you are ordinarily so careless or unlucky that you end up having losses every year or so. "The cost of absorbing small losses," as Hoffman puts it, "will pain you only for a minute."

Ask about premium discounts for burglar alarms, heat and smoke alarms, and automatic sprinklers if you have installed them in your home.

If you ever have a claim for over $5,000 and you're unhappy with the settlement the insurance company proposes, consider hiring a public adjuster to help you. An adjuster gets paid a commission of 10 or 15 percent of what is recovered. For names and more information, write to the National Association of Public Insurance Adjusters, 1613 Munsey Building, Baltimore, Md. 21202.

Finally, so you don't think you now know all there is to know about the subject of homeowners insurance, here's a frightfully difficult quiz:

TEST YOUR KNOWLEDGE OF HOMEOWNERS INSURANCE

1. On your property you have a garage that you rent out. If it is destroyed by fire, will the cost of replacing it be covered by your policy?

☐ yes ☐ no

Answer: *Yes, although homeowners policies do not generally cover buildings used for business purposes.*

2. Your purebred cat is killed in a fire at home. Will you get any reimbursement?

☐ yes ☐ no

Answer: *No.*

3. A neighbor yells at your 12-year-old son, and in retaliation the ill-tempered brat breaks the neighbor's picture window. Are you covered?

☐ yes ☐ no

Answer: *Yes, because damage caused intentionally by children under 13 is considered accidental. But the maximum you would be paid is $250, with a deductible.*

4. While visiting a friend, you sit in a chair that proceeds to break into smithereens. Will your friend's homeowners policy cover the loss?

☐ yes ☐ no

Answer: *No, but* your *policy will.*

5. You rent out a room in your house. The house burns to the ground. Will your homeowners insurance reimburse you for the lost rental income?

☐ yes ☐ no

Answer: *Yes.*

6. While your house is burning, it sets fire to a neighbor's house—and your neighbor has no insurance. If your neighbor sues, will your own homeowners policy cover any award?

☐ yes ☐ no

Answer: *Yes.*

EXHIBIT 5-3

LIMITS ON HOMEOWNERS INSURANCE

These are the limits to what most homeowners policies will pay on items you may own:

- Household goods and personal property: *50 percent of the insurance on the dwelling*
- Personal property away from home: *10 percent of the coverage on the contents at home*
- Securities, valuable papers, stamps: *$500*
- Money and coin collections: *$100*
- Boats and trailers, outboard motors: *$500*
- Other trailers and campers: *$500*
- Silverware, goldware, pewterware: *$1,000*
- Jewelry, furs, watches: *$500*
- Guns: *$1,000*

SURPRISING FACTS ABOUT HOMEOWNERS INSURANCE

7. Returning home from a vacation, you open the door of your freezer and a lot of spoiled food pours out onto the rug. A storm, it develops, has killed all the electric power in your area. Will your homeowners insurance policy reimburse you for the cost of the food?

☐ yes ☐ no

Answer: *No. But you may be covered for the stain on your rug.*

8. Which one of the following situations will *not* be covered by your homeowners policy? **A.** Your cigarette scorches a tabletop in someone else's home. **B.** Your 5-year-old pushes a playmate, injuring him. **C.** In a snit, you punch a visiting bill collector in the nose. **D.** Your 10-foot sailboat crashes into a canoe.

Answer: *C.*

9. A friend lends your wife a fur to wear to a party. Overnight your house is burglarized and the fur is swiped. Will your homeowners policy cover the loss?

☐ yes ☐ no

Answer: *Yes, probably. Many policies provide such coverage.*

10. You have a few hundred dollars in cash at home. When you try to spend it, a shopkeeper sees that it's counterfeit. Will your homeowners policy cover the loss?

☐ yes ☐ no

Answer: *Yes, probably. Many recent policies will. Losses caused by someone's illegal use of your credit card and by forgery may also be covered.*

11. While you are golfing, your cart slams into another golfer. Are you covered?

☐ yes ☐ no

Answer: *Yes. You are also covered if you own or rent an inboard- or inboard-outboard-powered boat of 50 horsepower or less; a sailboat less than 26 feet long; or an outboard-powered boat with no more than 25 horsepower.*

12. You own an old Victorian house. It's so stylish and ornate that insuring it for just 80 percent of its value would be exorbitant. But you don't want to insure it for less than 80 percent. What should you do?

Answer: *Consider an HO 8 policy. In case of loss, the house will be returned to serviceable condition, but not necessarily to the same high quality as the original.*

13. You have a floater on a Ming vase. The wind blows it over, and it breaks. Are you covered?

☐ yes ☐ no

Answer: *No, breakage is excluded. But for a little extra, you can buy breakage coverage.*

14. While soldering in your workshop, you start a fire. Are you covered?

☐ yes ☐ no

Answer: *Yes, so long as you were engaging in a hobby and not pursuing a sideline business.*

15. During a windstorm, your front door blows open and rain floods your living room. Are you covered for the damage?

☐ yes ☐ no

Answer: *No, not unless the door was so damaged by the storm that it let in the water.*

16. You rent an unfurnished cottage for the summer, bringing furniture from your permanent residence. If there's a fire, will your furniture be covered?

☐ yes ☐ no

Answer: *Yes, so long as the quarters are temporary.*

17. Someone carelessly throws some valuable papers of yours into a fireplace, where they are destroyed. Are you covered?

☐ yes ☐ no

Answer: *No. A fireplace fire is considered "friendly." If the fire had spread from the fireplace, it would have been different.*

SURPRISING FACTS ABOUT HOMEOWNERS INSURANCE

18. A diamond ring you own is filched from your hotel room. Does your homeowners policy cover the loss?

☐ yes ☐ no

Answer: *Yes, a homeowners policy would cover the first $500 of the loss, after a deductible. Any further loss would have to be covered by a floater.*

19. You spent $1,500 for a videocassette recorder that was destroyed in a fire. A comparable new model would cost $500. Will your homeowners insurance pay you $1,500 for a new one?

☐ yes ☐ no

Answer: *No, only $500.*

20. Fire destroys the moped in your garage. Does your homeowners insurance cover the damage?

☐ yes ☐ no

Answer: *No. Motorized vehicles would have to be covered by other policies.*

CHAPTER

6 MEASURING THE TAX ANGLES

Agreed, reading about federal income taxes tends to be painful, like having a tooth drilled by a clumsy dentist with a dull drill. Near the top of my own list of books never to take to a deserted island is *J.K. Lasser*'s *Your Income Tax*. With that in mind, I have constructed the following quiz to (1) challenge your knowledge, and (2) not be excruciatingly painful.

TEST YOUR TAX SAVVY

1. Termites feast on your house. May you deduct the loss on your income-tax return?

☐ yes ☐ no

Answer: *No, because the damage was not sudden. By the same token, you may not deduct for water damage when the water continuously seeped through a door or window. For a sudden and destructive loss, though, you can deduct the damage exceeding 10 percent of your adjusted gross income plus $100—if you itemize your deductions and don't recover on your insurance policy.*

2. Are you allowed to deduct property taxes and mortgage interest for a houseboat you live in, as well as a private home, summer home, cooperative, condominium, or mobile home?

☐ yes ☐ no

Answer: *Yes.*

3. The following comes from page 78 of an early edition of the 1982 *J.K. Lasser's Your Income Tax:* *

A doctor rents a 10-room apartment using three rooms for his office and seven rooms for his residence. Applying a percentage based on the ratio of rooms used as an office to the total rooms in the apartment, he deducts 30% (3/10) of the following expenses:

	Total	Office	Residence
Rent	$ 7,200	$2,160	$5,040
Light	600	180	420
Heat	1,000	300	700
Wages of domestic	2,000	600	1,400
	$10,800	$3,240	$7,560

$7,560 is deductible as a professional expense.

Is this true ☐ or false ☐?

Answer: *False. The $3,240 is deductible. (It was just a typographical error.) For any such expenses to be deductible, a portion of a taxpayer's residence must be used exclusively and regularly as (1) the taxpayer's place of business, or (2) a place used by clients in dealings with the taxpayer.*

4. You sell your house and, good grief, you lose money. May you deduct the loss?

☐ yes ☐ no

Answer: *No, not unless you were renting out the house.*

5. You spend $2,000 to install a wood-burning stove in your summer home. May you give yourself a credit for the cost, up to 15 percent ($300) for energy-saving equipment with a life of at least three years?

☐ yes ☐ no

Answer: *No, because a wood-burning stove doesn't qualify for an energy-saving tax credit, and it's a summer home, not your principal residence. (See Exhibit 6-1.) A tax credit, by the way, is better than a deduction—it reduces taxes you owe dollar for dollar.*

---
* Copyright © 1981 by J.K. Lasser Tax Institute. Reprinted by permission of Simon & Schuster, a Division of Gulf & Western Corporation.

MEASURING THE TAX ANGLES

EXHIBIT 6-1

ENERGY-SAVING TAX CREDITS

You can get tax credit for installing these energy-saving devices:

- Caulking for building joints and outside doors and windows
- Flue-opening modifications
- Furnace ignition systems replacing gas pilot lights
- Furnace replacement burners
- Insulation for ceilings, outside walls, floors, forced-air ducts, hot-water heaters (outside installation), roofs, steel doors, and storm windows
- Meters showing the cost of energy use
- Storm and thermal windows and doors
- Thermostats—clock thermostats or the kind having automatic set-back features
- Weather stripping for outside doors and windows

These are not eligible:

- Carpets
- Drapes
- Fluorescent lights
- Heat pumps
- Hydrogen-fueled equipment
- Outside siding
- Replacement boilers and furnaces
- Wood- or peat-burning stoves
- Wood paneling

You can also get tax credit for the following renewable-energy equipment:

- Geothermal energy equipment
- Geothermal wells
- Heat exchangers
- Plastic solar collectors
- Rock beds
- Solar collectors
- Solar-energy equipment
- Thermostats
- Wind-energy equipment
- Windmills

HOW TO BUY OR SELL YOUR HOME

6. You buy a house in which the previous owner had installed energy-saving devices costing $2,000. He also installed renewable-energy sources worth $10,000 (and took a tax credit of 40 percent). Are you entitled to a credit of up to $4,300 for *additional* energy-saving devices and renewable-energy sources?

☐ yes ☐ no

Answer: *Yes. And if you buy another home, you can collect credits of up to $4,300 again.*

7. One of the big breaks the government gives to us deserving homeowners is allowing us to postpone paying capital-gains taxes on profits from the main homes we buy and sell. What is the longest possible time we can postpone paying taxes on these gains? **A.** Until the last house we buy. **B.** Our heirs have to pay them after we die. **C.** They may never have to be repaid.

Answer: *C. After the homeowner dies, the postponed taxes are forgiven. The rules for postponing taxes in general are that the second house must be occupied within two years before or after the first house is sold, and the houses must be main residences, not vacation homes.*

8. If you build a new main house, can you get any renewable-energy-source tax credits?

☐ yes ☐ no

Answer: *Yes, and all existing houses are also eligible. But to qualify for the tax credit for energy-saving devices, houses must have been substantially completed before April 20, 1977.*

9. You exchange your home, valued at $20,000 more than you paid for it, for another home that's worth just as much as yours. Are you entitled to defer your $20,000 gain?

☐ yes ☐ no

Answer: *Yes, an exchange is treated like a sale.*

10. You spend $10,000 fighting in court to defend your title to your house. May you add this cost to the basis of your house in figuring the capital gains when you sell?

☐ yes ☐ no

MEASURING THE TAX ANGLES

Answer: *Yes, usually. Along with improvements (not repairs) and other expenses in acquiring your home, like legal fees and title insurance you paid for yourself.*

11. Just before putting your house up for sale, you have a new kitchen installed. In figuring the possible capital gains, may you deduct the kitchen's cost from the sales price as a "fix-up cost"?

☐ yes   ☐ no

Answer: *No, it's an improvement added to the cost basis of the house. So you don't lose the cost even if the sale doesn't go through—as you might with a fix-up cost. You may deduct fix-up costs incurred within 90 days of the sale and paid within 30 days after the sale only if the sale goes through. You can also deduct expenses like real-estate commissions and legal fees.*

12. Another big break the government lavishes upon us is the $125,000 tax exemption (up from $100,000, which is up from $35,000) for homeowners 55 years old or older who have lived in their main residences for three of the five years preceding the

EXHIBIT 6-2

IMPROVEMENTS VERSUS REPAIRS

Here's how the Internal Revenue Service explains the difference between improvements, which may be used to increase the tax basis of your home, and repairs, which may not:

Improvements. A home improvement materially adds to the value of your home, appreciably prolongs its useful life, or adapts it to new uses. Putting in a recreation room in your unfinished basement, adding another bathroom or bedroom, putting up a fence, putting in new plumbing or wiring, installing a new roof, or paving your driveway are improvements that are added to the basis of your home.

Repairs. A repair merely maintains your home in an ordinary, efficient operating condition. It doesn't add value to your home, or appreciably prolong its life. Repainting inside or outside, fixing your gutters or floors, mending leaks, and plastering and replacing broken window panes are examples of repairs.

HOW TO BUY OR SELL YOUR HOME

EXHIBIT 6-3

CHECKLIST OF HOME IMPROVEMENTS

You can reduce the taxes you may owe on any profits from the sale of your house by adding the cost of improvements to the original price you paid. Keep all bills and receipts. This checklist can help you remember any improvements—*not* repairs—that you have made.

IMPROVEMENTS TO THE HOUSE
Structural work
- ☐ Installation of louvers and screen vents in the attic
- ☐ Upgrading of roofing, gutters, or exterior covering of house
- ☐ Installation of awnings, sunshades, shutters, blinds, storm doors, storm windows, or screens
- ☐ Upgrading of interiors, such as installation or improvement of fireplace with major brick, stone, cement, or plastering work
- ☐ New doors, new windows, or acoustic ceilings
- ☐ Strengthening of structure with steel girders, reinforcing rods, or floor jacks
- ☐ Work done on the foundation to eliminate water seepage and settling

Additions and finishing
- ☐ Rooms
- ☐ Porches
- ☐ Closets, laundry chutes, or dumbwaiters
- ☐ Attic and basement improvements

Built-in furnishings
- ☐ Addition of permanently placed units, such as chests, cabinets, or shelving
- ☐ Installation of permanent floor covering

Equipment
- ☐ Built-in stereo equipment or hobby machinery
- ☐ Intercoms
- ☐ Fire or burglar alarms
- ☐ Garbage disposal or dishwasher
- ☐ Built-in freezer or refrigerator
- ☐ Additional stoves
- ☐ Sauna
- ☐ Elevator

Source: *Medical Economics* magazine.

Electrical wiring
☐ Installation of new power lines or lighting fixtures
☐ Additional outlets or switches

Plumbing, heating, and air-conditioning
☐ New or additional plumbing fixtures, sinks, laundry tubs, or water softeners
☐ Piping, tanks, pumps, or wells
☐ Upgrading of heating systems
☐ Installation of air-conditioning units, a central air-conditioning system, attic fans, air humidifiers and dehumidifiers, or air-filtration systems

IMPROVEMENTS TO THE GROUNDS
Landscaping
☐ Enlargement of lawn area
☐ Addition or removal of trees or shrubbery
☐ Resurfacing of land areas or installation of drain tiles or other equipment to eliminate problems associated with the property's water drainage
☐ Addition to or redesign of decorative pools or arbors

Paving and surfaces
☐ Blacktopping or other improvements to driveway
☐ Laying or extension of walks or curbs
☐ Addition to or enlargement of patios

Recreational facilities
☐ Installation of an outdoor swimming pool as well as other, related facilities
☐ Tennis, badminton, or other game courts
☐ Children's playground equipment

Equipment
☐ Outdoor sound systems, lighting, or lampposts
☐ Barbecue pits or incinerators
☐ Underground sprinkler system

Structures
☐ Addition or removal of fences, walls, or trellises
☐ Improvement of garages, carports, tool sheds, stables, barns, greenhouses, or other outbuildings

sale. This exclusion is a once-in-a-lifetime deal, so you may decide to cancel your first exclusion and use another one. How long do you have to change your mind? **A.** One year from the due date of the return filed for the year of the sale. **B.** Three years from the due date. **C.** Indefinitely.

Answer: B. *You have three years from the due date of the return to revoke your first exclusion and choose one for another house.*

13. A married couple is entitled to only one exclusion. Suppose a widower and a widow marry, and each has claimed the exclusion before. Must one spouse now pay a capital-gains tax on the profits?

☐ yes ☐ no

Answer: *No, thank heavens.*

14. One spouse is 55, the other 13. (No, this isn't a French novel.) Are the two of them together entitled to the exclusion if they fulfill the other rules?

☐ yes ☐ no

Answer: *Yes.*

15. A woman sells a house and claims part of the $125,000 exclusion. She marries a man who has never claimed the exclusion. They buy a house and sell it five years later for a juicy profit—$125,000. How much can the *man* exclude from taxes? **A.** All. **B.** Half. **C.** None.

Answer: *C. And yes, it seems unfair that he isn't entitled to half, but he should have made a more judicious choice of brides. Or perhaps they should have bought the house as tenants in common instead of tenants by the entirety. Certainly they should have checked with their lawyer first.*

16. You rent out your second home for fewer than 15 days during the year. May you deduct a portion of your expenses, such as maintenance costs?

☐ yes ☐ no

Answer: *No, but don't complain. None of your profit is taxed.*

OWNING

CHAPTER

7 SMART AND DUMB HOME IMPROVEMENTS

Let's say you have a spare $5,000 or $10,000 and want to put it into your house. Of course, it would be just hunky-dory if you choose improvements so shrewdly that, come time to sell, you get your money back—and then some. So what should you do?

- Add a new bathroom—or build a wet bar in your basement?
- Install a rooftop solar heater—or bolster the attic insulation?
- Remodel the kitchen—or add a third garage?

More and more Americans are making such choices these days, because the United States is in the midst of a home-improvement renaissance. With mortgage rates so high, many homeowners are finding themselves under house arrest: There just aren't many buyers around. So homeowners are building up, not moving up.

Granted, not every home improvement *must* pay off directly by increasing the selling price of a house. Some flashy items, like automatic garage-door openers, just may help a house sell faster. Other improvements may add a certain zest to the homeowner's life while doing nothing to add to or detract from the house's value—like a darkroom. In other words, the homeowner should not feel constricted by the consideration of whether an improvement will pay off or not.

Still, other things being equal, it's better to be slightly richer than poorer. And a homeowner who wants to install an improvement that will help his house appreciate should begin by heeding several generalizations.

GOLDEN RULES
The future value of a home improvement depends on one's *neighborhood*. When buyers tell a real-estate agent that they want to buy a $200,000 house, the agent takes them to neighborhoods where $200,000 houses are the rule. People hankering after $200,000 houses want to be surrounded by $200,000 houses, not by ugly, decaying $100,000 houses. So if a homeowner has a $200,000 house in a $200,000 neighborhood, he should be wary of making improvements that will lift his house out of the neighborhood's range. "The basic mistake people make is to overimprove for their location," says George H. Brenner, a Realtor in Westport, Mass. By the same token, if someone has a $160,000 house in a $200,000 area, he can hardly go wrong with home improvements.

The *region of the country* has a bearing on home improvements, too. Swimming pools are the fashion wherever it's warm almost all year long—typically, the Sun Belt states—but are scarce in the East, except with ritzy houses. In the West, wall-to-wall carpeting is popular; in the East it isn't, possibly because of the attractive hardwood floors common there.

The *estimated selling price* of a house matters. When people buy houses for $100,000 and up, they expect certain accoutrements (like garbage disposals) they don't expect in less expensive houses. Tastes also change in the $100,000-and-up range. According to a poll published by *Professional Builder* magazine in December of 1981, a "great room"—combination living room and dining room—appeals to the low-cost housing crowd, but is anathema to mansion dwellers, who long for formal dining and living rooms.

A final consideration: The *tax laws* favor home improvements—especially if the homeowner is young, if he is planning to stay put for quite some time, and if the improvements themselves save energy.

THE BEST IMPROVEMENTS
A remodeled kitchen may be the safest single home improvement. But even a kitchen can be overimproved. Few buyers,

SMART AND DUMB HOME IMPROVEMENTS

except those looking at homes for $100,000 and up, expect built-in microwave ovens. And even in the $100,000-and-up bracket, less than 40 percent of buyers expect to find trash compactors.

What well-to-do homeowners *do* favor in the way of kitchens: a dishwasher, fluorescent lights, a garbage disposal, one-handle faucets (69.7 percent versus 24.6 percent for two-handle faucets), and stainless-steel sinks over enamel/porcelain sinks.

After the kitchen comes the bathroom. "A sparkling bathroom sells a house," says Joseph H. Lumpkin, a Realtor in Columbia, S.C. Installing a new bathroom is a particularly good idea when the house is short of them, the rule being that there should be one and a half bathrooms for every two bedrooms. A two-story house, though, needs at least a half bath on the first floor and a full one upstairs. A bath off the master bedroom is also a good bet. In general, buyers expect a minimum of two full bathrooms. But a sizable minority would accept one and a half. Those buyers looking for more expensive homes tend to expect two and a half bathrooms.

Other features that well-to-do buyers expect in bathrooms: linen storage cabinets, exhaust fans, tub/shower doors, ceramic tile walls and floors, two-bowl vanities, colored fixtures, dressing areas, and safety features like railings.

But, like kitchens, bathrooms can be overimproved. "I mean, you can have one of those Grecian-type tubs to sit and soak in," says George Brenner. "It's got a separate shower and it's got a button you push and the lights dim and a scantily clad girl comes out and gives you a massage. But the family that's looking the house over may be a minister and his wife with three or four kids."

Other safe bets include first-floor family rooms, especially those near the kitchen so that the cook can watch the children. Also consider a second garage, not necessarily for a car but for storage space. Forget about three-car garages. A distinctive foyer is worthwhile.

In the years to come, as mentioned, large living quarters may be passé, but right now homebuyers welcome an enlarged dining room and living room as well as a third bedroom. But not necessarily a fourth bedroom. A large minority—probably today's smaller families—even prefer a larger master suite or special-interest room to a third bedroom.

FIREPLACES AND ENERGY-SAVERS

And thus we come to the mysterious case of the fireplace. Fireplaces rank up there with kitchens and bathrooms as safe bets, even though they squander large amounts of energy. "Fireplaces just suck heat right out of your house," says Harlan C. Williams, a Realtor in Newark, Del. "Especially if you have to leave the damper open at night while the embers go out." Still, as Williams notes, fireplaces definitely sell houses.

By and large, there is growing interest in energy-savers among buyers, especially among the well-educated. But right now they don't add much to a home's value. People still buy houses because they fall in love with them, and they don't fall in love with them because of their solar water heaters. The best reason to get energy-saving devices is so that they can save you money directly, along with giving you tax credits. A solar water heater, though, is inadvisable because it tends to rust away quickly. One builder says, "It wouldn't be much better than having a 1959 Plymouth nailed to your roof." Overall, the only energy-savers likely to prompt buyers to pay more are storm windows.

THE BIGGEST MISTAKES

The *Professional Builder* poll found that full basements are popular everywhere except Texas, Louisiana, Arkansas, and Oklahoma. Still, basement improvements—a wet bar, for example—are usually unwise. Homeowners don't spend much time in their basements anymore.

"In the first house I owned," says Leo J. Sheridan Jr., a Realtor in Winnetka, Ill., "I improved the basement. I paneled it, divided it, and everything else. I sold the house six months later, and never got my money back. The second house, all I did was have the kids go down and paint the walls. Then I had them decorate them with their own drawings. The only limitation I put on was no four-letter words."

Aluminum siding probably won't return your money at the sale. *Professional Builder* found that only 10 percent of buyers prefer aluminum siding, while 46.6 percent go for brick masonry and 17.3 percent for wood siding. To many people, wood siding simply looks better than aluminum. And wood shakes and shingles (shakes are cut by hand, shingles by machine) and vinyl siding are even less appealing to most people than aluminum siding.

Other features of a house that are *not* especially popular with the average buyer include outdoor lighting, concrete patios, decking for the patio, lawn sprinkling systems, built-in bookshelves, screened porches, central vacuums, greenhouses, intercom systems, and water softeners. Generally you won't get back the money you spend on frills—bidets, whirlpool showers, saunas, tennis courts, and gazebos.

The basic rule on home improvements comes from Leo Sheridan: "Don't do anything drastic." It may be your house now, but someday you may want it to be somebody else's.

Harlan Williams tells the tale of a family transferred to Newark, Del., by the Ronson Company. "It was a new house they bought," he says, "and the wife came down here and picked out the colors to go with the house. I don't know where the woman's head was, but she picked out the darnedest things, very vivid lavender and a very vivid Kelly green for the dining room, and a mustard yellow for the den, and just about every room you went into was bang, bang, bang, it just hit you. The first thing you saw was the color and not the room.

"Well, lo and behold, the fellow was transferred again before they ever moved into the house. The company lived up to its agreement, and took the house over from him and turned it over to us for resale. Well, we couldn't get people interested in it because of the colors.

"The man from Ronson handling the resale would call once in a while, and finally I told him, 'You know, you're probably going to smile at this, or get mad, but we're having trouble selling that house because of the colors.' And he said, 'That's ridiculous.' His whole attitude was that 'You people are not doing your job.' So I said, 'When are you going to be in Newark?' He said, 'I'll be down there in a week and a half.'

"So we went out to look at the house at 11 one morning and he walked into the entrance hall, looked around, peered up the steps, and said, 'Paint the son of a bitch.'

"We had the house sold in about two weeks."

THE TAX ANGLES

Even if you have been rash enough to install a regulation soccer field in your backyard, you may eventually wind up not doing badly. The cost of any improvement, as we saw, may be added to the basis of your house when you sell and thus reduce any tax on your profits.

This doesn't mean that you should go haywire in improving your home. First, capital gains are taxed leniently. Second, you might *never* have to pay capital-gains taxes on the sale of your home. You might keep on buying expensive house after expensive house, thus postponing the taxes. Or, when you or your spouse reaches 55, you may qualify for a $125,000 exclusion of capital gains from taxes.

What this means is that, financially, the best time to make improvements is when you're far under 55, when there's still a lot of time for you to owe the government taxes from the sale of your house.

All in all, the home-improvement deduction is worth keeping in mind. The deduction is, happily, for the full cost of whatever improvement you have installed, without depreciation. If you paid $3,000 for that hideously moth-eaten carpet 15 years ago, you may still lower your capital gains by $3,000 in figuring out what you owe.

CHAPTER

8 HOW TO TRAP A HOMING PIGEON

> "As a temporary first-aid measure, hang a few pictures over worn areas. It is not likely that buyers will look behind pictures to see if there are any marks."
> —*How to Sell Your House for More Than It's Worth,* by Jerry Pennington and Fred G. Schultz, p. 31

> "If pictures seem hung in strange spots around the room, they may be hiding a defect. Don't be embarrassed to look behind them."
> —*Ibid.,* p. 141

People buying houses have different dream homes in mind. But people selling houses all dream of the same buyer—someone who will pay an extravagant asking price. The likeliest homing pigeons are young couples and out-of-towners unfamiliar with the local housing market. In California, the real-estate crowd calls such innocents "buyers from the East."

Home sellers who obdurately wait for a buyer from the East sometimes never find one and wind up making a distress sale. By and large, a homeowner should aim for a quick sale, one that will take him no more than several months. What that might call for, besides a reasonable asking price, is hiring a good broker, putting the house on the market at the right time, and making appropriate improvements and repairs.

A portion of this chapter was reprinted from the April 1975 issue of *Money* magazine by special permission; © 1975, Time Inc.

THE POKING PARADE

A quick sale spares you that parade of people poking and sniffing through your house, flushing toilets, making slighting remarks and dumb comments—to cite one actual instance, that the trouble with asbestos siding is that it burns readily.

A quick sale may also be the best bet financially. It helps protect you against owning a new house before your old one is sold. The possible consequences: You continue paying for the mortgage and for property taxes, insurance, and utility costs on your old shack; you may have to borrow at a thumpingly high interest rate (even if you can borrow against the equity in your old house) for the down payment on your new palace.

Looking at an unsold empty house, some buyers will reasonably conclude that out of desperation the owner is ready to accept an unreasonably low offer. Other buyers will make low bids simply because vacant rooms are depressing. "An empty house," wrote the 19th-century novelist Samuel Butler, "is like a stray dog or a body from which life has departed." By comparison, an occupied house recently put up for sale is a fresh rose among wilting flowers. Agents rush to show new listings to a backlog of buyers who have not yet found the house they like. The faster a house sells, after all, the better-paid the agent is for his time.

A reasonable price is the main catalyst for a quick sale. Too many homeowners, fatuously optimistic about the jack their houses have built, price themselves out of the market. Usually, the best way to set a reasonable asking price is to find out what buyers have recently been paying for similar houses nearby.

EXPENSIVE THRILLS

Call in three or four real-estate agents and ask them what price to shoot for and why. Concentrate on the typical prices mentioned, not on a thrillingly high suggestion, advises Bart K. Wickstrum, director of residential sales for Homequity, a company that relocates employees. Some agents deliberately overshoot the mark in hopes of appealing to your greed.

If your local housing market is slow or your house is unusual—a two-story house in a sea of ranches, for example—consider hiring an appraiser, at a cost of $150 or so. Look in the Yellow Pages, under Real Estate Appraisers or Appraisers, for someone with offices nearby who will know the reputation of the school system and which parts of town are the most or least desirable. Or ask your local commercial bank or savings and loan association for names. Make sure that the appraiser has certification from a professional association. The two biggest are the American Institute of Real Estate Appraisers and the Society of Real Estate Appraisers. "A lot of people who call themselves appraisers are bilking the public," says Alvin L. Wagner Jr. of Flossmoor, Ill., a member of the governing council of the Institute. "Some of them appraise a house without ever going inside."

After deciding what price you can reasonably get for your house, add on 5 to 10 percent for bargaining. If you want a quick sale, leave it at 5 percent. If you're willing to wait awhile, tack on 10 percent. You might be lucky enough to encounter a buyer from the East.

The best time to put your house on the market is spring and early summer. Many buyers want to purchase a house in the spring and move in during the summer, so as not to interrupt their children's schooling. Fall is the next-best time to sell. Alvin Wagner says that when he evaluates residences he is usually "bullish early in the year, bearish late in the year."

WHEN DETAILS ARE DECISIVE
Before showing your house to customers, apply the traditional home remedies. To make a house look more spacious, get rid of whatever has been cluttering closets and storage areas. Hold a garage sale, lawn sale, tag sale—whatever you call it in your area—and junk whatever doesn't sell. Have windows cleaned, floors swept, the house aired. To keep the house tidy, hide half the children's toys and spread scatter rugs over floors that tend to get dirty easily.

A buyer typically looks at 15 different houses. He may wind up torn between two of them. One house might be 20 years old with a fireplace, a two-car garage, and walk-in closets, but an older kitchen, no first-floor bathroom, and a suspicious damp spot in the basement. The other house might be 12 years old with a modern kitchen and first-floor bathroom but a one-car garage, small closets, no fireplace, and a suspicious damp spot in the attic. When choices are difficult, little things like dirty windows can mean a lot.

Don't neglect to have leaky faucets fixed, faded walls repainted or repapered, carpets cleaned, and other minor alterations made. Real-estate people say that when a buyer estimates how much it would cost to have, say, a light fixture replaced, he overestimates by 100 to 150 percent. By all means, spend $200 to spruce up your house if a buyer might think it would cost him $400 to $500; he might otherwise deduct that much from his bid. If you do choose to redecorate, choose white, beige, or other neutral colors that won't clash with a prospective buyer's furnishings.

One major project you should consider is having the outside of your house repainted. A house should have what agents call "curb appeal"; otherwise, prospective buyers may simply drive up and drive on.

Most other changes that cost a lot of money—having new carpets laid, or central air-conditioning installed—are risky. If you are seriously thinking of improvements merely to help your house sell faster, ask several companies for written estimates, so you can show an interested buyer what the lowest cost would be. As we have seen, the tax laws make certain improvements attractive by reducing the capital-gains tax that people might have to pay on their profits from selling a house.

Repairs and decorating costs to help you sell a house—so-called fix-up costs—do not qualify as improvements. But they, too, can sometimes reduce a capital-gains tax. For tax purposes, fix-up costs can be subtracted from the amount realized on your first house. You must make the repairs no more than 90 days before you sign a contract to sell the house (another incentive for a quick sale) and pay for them no later than 30 days after the sale is closed. You can subtract the cost of materials for repairs you do yourself, but not the cost of your labor.

FEAR OF FLYING ANTS

Years ago, lawyers advised sellers to forget about making major alterations that could not be seen and admired. Even if you had seen horrid antlike creatures flying around your basement, you were not counseled to have your house termite-proofed. It was up to the buyer to beware. Today, the buyer need not beware so much. Courts have been holding sellers responsible for significant hidden defects.

Recently a family that purchased a house in New Jersey won the state Supreme Court's permission to sue the seller for allegedly permitting visits to the house only when all the lights were on, so cockroaches would remain in hiding.

Another argument for candor is that it's not always possible to conceal the need for repairs. If a buyer hires an inspector and learns that the basement leaks, you may lose the sale.

A standard piece of advice for sellers is to keep away from prospective buyers and allow only the agents to talk to them. One Connecticut homeowner, asked whether there were many children in the neighborhood, enthusiastically replied that there were scores of them. The prospective buyer had no children and didn't want other people's children whooping through the neighborhood. No sale. But George Snowden Jr., a staff member of the National Association of Real Estate Brokers, thinks that an owner who knows his house inside out might volunteer impressive information, such as that the floorboards are anchored by wooden pegs, not by nails.

Most sellers would perhaps not balk at a little window dressing, such as a fire in the fireplace, pleasant music playing on the stereo, and brighter bulbs in the light fixtures. But some might choke on such agents' euphemisms as calling a cramped house "cozy," or old-fashioned fixtures "charming," or a treeless plot "sunny." In talking to newlyweds, perhaps only salesmad agents would unblushingly stress positive words like "privacy" and "independence," and avoid negative words like "duty" and "security," as motivational researchers suggest. Still other sellers might gag at the advice given in a 1973 book, *For Sale by Owner,* to start baking bread before visitors come, just for the aroma. "You may not be a baker but you can buy frozen bread dough at the supermarket and turn on the oven."

Manipulating house-hunters may be reprehensible, but it is nothing new. In an 1884 issue of *Leisure Hour* magazine, an English "literary man" named Charles Wilton tells of looking for a house to rent in London. The experience taught him "how much mendacity can be hung upon a thread of truth." One house he was shown supposedly had a conservatory. When Wilton asked to see it, the woman in charge threw open a door to an outdoor path. "Does this lead to the conservatory?" he asked. "No, sir. Oh, no," she replied. "We call this the conservatory. You might roof it in, you see, sir."

CHOOSING A BROKER

The heaviest expense of selling a house is almost always the broker's commission. It typically ranges from 6 to 10 percent of the sale price.

If you decide to use a broker, choose someone who impresses you with his knowledge and integrity. He will probably impress buyers the same way. Check to see which broker advertises the most houses for sale in your vicinity. Telephone several banks nearby and ask the mortgage officers which brokers they have many dealings with. Give preference to a broker who belongs to the National Association of Realtors, which has high ethical standards.

TYPES OF LISTINGS

There are three types of listing arrangements you can make with a broker.

1. *The open listing.* You can hire as many brokers to sell your house as you want. Whoever brings in a ready, willing, and able buyer collects the full commission. And if you find a buyer yourself, you don't owe anyone a commission. In theory, an open listing is wonderful. "But unless it's a very salable and reasonably priced house," says Thomas R. Eldridge, a broker in Ridgewood, N.J., "many brokers won't be interested." For brokers and their salesmen, selling a house on an open listing may mean a lot of time and effort, possibly for nothing.

2. *Exclusive agency.* Only one broker can sell your house. That broker need not allow other brokers to find possible buyers. But if you find your own buyer, you usually won't owe the broker a commission.

Just bear in mind that giving a broker an exclusive agency may result in your taking longer to sell your house and getting a lower price than if your house had been shown by all the brokers in your community through a multiple-listing system.

To minimize such a possibility, give an exclusive agency only to "the hottest broker in town," says Walter Kantrowitz in his book *How to Be Your Own Lawyer—Sometimes*. The hottest broker is likely to be the one with the biggest and best ads in the newspapers.

3. *The exclusive right to sell.* This is the most popular arrangement. You list your house through one broker, and he lets other brokers show the house through the multiple-listing system. The listing broker is automatically entitled to a portion of the commission—usually 50 percent—while the broker who finds a ready, willing, and able buyer gets the balance. (Of course, if the listing broker finds the buyer, he gets it all.)

Ordinarily, the listing broker will work hardest to sell your house because he wants to earn the full commission. He will bring around the ripest prospects—buyers who have sold their own houses already, buyers who have turned down everything they've seen so far and simply can't afford to be too choosy anymore, and so on.

Here are some provisions that should be included in a contract with a broker:

- After 60 to 90 days, the contract should expire. Some brokers don't really start pushing a house until the last minute, so the less time you give them in the contract, the less time you may have to wait for a sale.
- Insist on not paying any commission until your house actually changes hands at the closing. Otherwise you may owe a commission even if, at the last moment, you decide not to sell after all.
- If your house is to go into multiple listing, persuade the listing broker to accompany other brokers' salesmen through your house, if they show it while you're out. Salesmen have been known to be careless. In one case, a visitor left a door open in the dead of winter, causing the water pipes inside the house to freeze and burst.
- Have the listing broker agree that no green part-timers will show your house. A part-timer may receive a bountiful offer on your house and leave the information in the car from one weekend to the next. Or he may grievously mislead a buyer about your property. In one instance, a salesman told a buyer that a house had a working fireplace. The fireplace was actually only for show. On a chill night, the new owner proudly gathered his family around and lit a hearth- and heartwarming fire in the decorative fireplace. Before the fire was out, soot blanketed the room and a valuable rug was scorched.

THE BINDING BINDER

Comes the glorious day when a ready, willing, and able buyer arrives on stage. Your salesman may want you to sign a binder, or preliminary contract, and accept the buyer's earnest money. Be dubious. Lawyer Stephen Seldin thinks it much wiser—especially for the seller—to insist on consulting a lawyer and getting a full-fledged four-page contract, not a flimsy one-page contract. (A typical binder is illustrated in Exhibit 8-1.)

PROPOSAL TO PURCHASE MEMORANDUM

hereinafter referred to as Buyer, hereby authorizes .... to present the following proposal to purchase premises situate: ....

for the sum of .... $..................

SUMS PAID HEREWITH .... $..................

BUYER AGREES TO MAKE AN ADDITIONAL PAYMENT OF .... $..................
at time of signing of Agreement of Sale and Buyer and Seller agree to execute Agreement of Sale on or before ....

BUYER HEREBY AGREES TO PAY .... $..................
in cash or certified check at time of final settlement.

THE AGREEMENT of SALE shall provide the same is subject to Buyer obtaining a
☐ VA, ☐ FHA, ☐ Conventional mortgage maturing in .... years in the amount of $..................
OR

that title to be conveyed shall be subject to existing mortgage with approximate balance of .... $..................
maturing in approximately .... years at a rate of ....%.

FINAL SETTLEMENT is to be held on or before .... at ....M.,
at the office of ....,
or at the office of any reputable Title Company, as shall be provided under said Agreement of Sale.

THIS PROPOSAL TO PURCHASE is made on the following Terms and Conditions:

EXHIBIT 8-1

THIS PROPOSAL TO PURCHASE INCLUDES all fixtures permanently attached to the building or buildings herein described; and appurtenances. The following items now in use or in storage at premises are also included in sale price: all screens and storm sash, screen and storm doors, shades and/or blinds, shutters, electrical fixtures, plumbing and heating equipment and kitchen range; together with all items of landscaping and planting. ALSO INCLUDED OR EXCLUDED ARE:

IT IS ALSO UNDERSTOOD AND AGREED under the Agreement of Sale that Sellers shall provide Buyers with a negative termite report, or be responsible for the arrest of such activity if prevailing.

THIS PROPOSAL TO PURCHASE has been received by .... as agents for the Seller and subject to the approval of the Seller. If this Proposal to Purchase is not approved by the Seller within .... days, then said payment herewith made will be returned to Buyer.

This instrument is only a stage in the transaction until an Agreement of Sale is executed between the parties.
IN WITNESS WHEREOF, the parties hereto have hereunto set their hands and seals.

		Date ....
.... hereby	BUYER	Signed .... (LS)
acknowledges receipt of the above-mentioned sums paid		Signed .... (LS)
herewith.		Address ....
By:		.... PHONE ....
COOPERATING BROKER:		APPROVED:
....		Date ....
Phone:	SELLER	Signed .... (LS)
		Signed .... (LS)

One reason is that binders are binding. And if you, the seller, change your mind, you may not have an out. "I've seen it happen a couple of times," says Seldin, "that an older woman sits down at closing time and suddenly refuses to sign any papers. Suddenly the thought of leaving her home and her friends is too oppressive, and she'll want to back out. And I've seen it happen that after one buyer offers a binder on a house, another buyer comes along with a higher price for the house—but the seller is stuck with the lower bid."

Recently Andrew and Lillian Brandwein of Queens, N.Y., put their house up for sale, and their broker quickly brought them a binder and $250 earnest money. The Brandweins signed. The next day, they changed their minds and returned the check. The buyer sued, and eight months later a judge *ordered* the Brandweins to sell.

Another reason a seller should avoid a binder is that, at contract time, things can get ticklish and complicated. If the buyer wants the sale contingent on his selling his own house, how much time should the seller give? Or how much time should the seller give if the buyer wants the sale contingent on his getting enough mortgage money and satisfactory terms? These questions should have been settled as early as possible.

If you simply cannot resist accepting a binder, write on it: "Subject to the approval of my lawyer." Demand a sizable amount of earnest money, like $500, to dissuade the buyer from backing out. And don't take your house off the market. Keep showing it and keep advertising it, meanwhile explaining to interested buyers that sales negotiations are under way.

CHAPTER

9 THREE WAYS TO KNOCK DOWN A BROKER'S COMMISSION

A few years back, a physician in El Paso was trying to sell his house himself. A real-estate salesman, noticing the "For Sale" sign on the lawn, dropped in and urged the doctor's wife to list the house with his discount agency, Action Real Estate. His employer, he told her, charged only a $650 fee, as opposed to the prevailing commission rate in El Paso, 7 percent. (Today Action's fee is 2 percent of the selling price.) The doctor and his wife mulled it over, decided it sounded fishy, and said No.

So they put their house into the hands of a regular broker. That broker turned the house over to the local multiple-listing service. A month later, the house sold for $56,000.

The doctor paid the listing broker $3,920. That broker had to fork over part of the commission to a second broker, the one who had actually brought in the buyer. The second broker was—you guessed it—the man from Action Real Estate. In other words, the doctor had made a $3,270 mistake by mistrusting the discount broker.

Today, you don't have to pay a top-dollar commission when you sell your house—and you don't have to sell it yourself to beat the game. There are three other ways to lower a broker's commission.

(1) FOR-SALE-BY-OWNER AGENCIES

These agencies are the newest wrinkle in bringing down brokers' fees. As a rule, they do everything but show buyers through your home. They help you price a house realistically; they advertise it; they handle the closing. Their fees are delightfully low. Unfortunately, not many work with regular brokers on multiple-listing services. And lately, along with regular brokers, they have fallen upon hard times.

The Home Sellers Center in Buffalo, N.Y., charges 3 percent of the selling price. But if the seller doesn't want to show his own house, the agency will do it and charge an additional 1 percent. There's also a flat fee of $95 at the time of listing. If the house is sold by another broker on the multiple-listing system, the fee is 4 percent. At one time, says the broker, Mary Gore, there were eight agencies; now there's only one.

4-3-2-1 Realty in Falls Church, Va., collects 1 percent of the selling price if the owner sells to someone who saw the place before it was listed with the agency; 2 percent if the seller shows the house; 3 percent if the agency does everything, including showing the house to buyers; and 4 percent if the agency has to split the commission with another broker on the multiple-listing system. "We're not doing great," says broker Alice Maher, "but we're not doing any worse." 4-3-2-1 has been in business since 1973.

Suburban Home Advisors in Rockville, Md., charges 2 percent of the selling price. If the seller wants to go to multiple listing—something that has happened only rarely—the fee goes to 6 percent.

A few years ago, when Dennis L. Zilavy, M.D., a resident, had to move to Alaska, he sold his house in Phoenix through Continental Real Estate Consultants, a local by-owner agency that charged a flat $350 (now $950). Dr. Zilavy says that Continental was especially helpful in following up with potential buyers—telephoning them about any objections they had, for instance. Although the agency advertised his house, Dr. Zilavy ran ads of his own because he was in a hurry to move.

All in all, the doctor showed 75 people through his house, 15 of them (naturally) salesmen trying to get a regular listing. In his opinion, having to stay around the house was the main drawback. Still, the place sold in five weeks for what he had been asking: $72,000. Dr. Zilavy saved $4,690, based on the 7 percent commission that he would have had to pay.

THREE WAYS TO KNOCK DOWN A BROKER'S COMMISSION

"Maybe once you're making big bucks you don't have to bother with a by-owner agency," Dr. Zilavy says. "But I needed the money. And I don't mind getting almost $5,000 for a little bit of work. It wasn't *that* bad."

The next time he sells a house, the young doctor won't even use an agency at all. "This was my first time selling a house," he says, "and I felt that I needed a consultant. Now I've learned enough to sell a house by myself."

(2) DISCOUNT BROKERS

Brokers have always been willing to cut their commissions. They just haven't wanted it widely known. "They would reduce their rates privately and disclaim it publicly," says William Becker, a real-estate marketing consultant who teaches at the New York University School of Continuing Education and Extension Services.

The difference nowadays is that some brokers advertise their knocked-down commissions. The line that brokers used to hand out about the inviolability of their 6 or 7 percent commissions has proved a Maginot Line.

There are three main reasons that brokers will lower their fees, especially on certain expensive houses.

First, many brokers themselves acknowledge the unfairness of charging the same percentage to sell a rundown house in a crummy neighborhood—a house that may take many months to unload—and an attractive, reasonably priced dwelling in a fine neighborhood that, even in these abnormal times, might sell in a weekend or two.

Second, the courts have come down hard on brokers who stick together on 6 or 7 percent commissions. As a result, some brokers are eager to add variety to their commission schedules. "Now's a great time to negotiate," says Joan Haberle, former head of the New Jersey Real Estate Commission.

Third, these days a lot of brokers are starving. Most are desperate to get any sort of listing.

You find discount brokers the same way you find by-owner agencies: by browsing through newspaper real-estate ads and the display ads in the Yellow Pages. The ads may say: "Ask about our low selling fee," "Old-time commission rates," "Our low commissions mean low prices," and so forth.

Generally, discount brokers' commissions are one percentage point below the rates other brokers in the area charge. One

Long Island discount broker recalls charging only 3 percent recently: "The house was in excellent condition, it showed well, it was decorated beautifully. It had good landscaping, it was in a good area, and it was priced reasonably."

Bob Park, who owns Action Real Estate in El Paso, has been running a discount business for several years now. "Other brokers bad-mouth us," he says. "They probably told that doctor who didn't list with us, but whose house we sold anyway, that we were disreputable." Still, says Park, over 25 agents for other companies have purchased personal dwellings through his agency, for themselves or for members of their families. Recently Park and a group of sellers sued the local multiple-listing service and 65 brokers on charges of price-fixing.

(3) BARGAINING WITH BROKERS

Even if you deal with a full-service broker who doesn't advertise a cut-rate commission, you may be able to bargain him down. You have a good case if your house is spic-and-span, situated in a good area, and—above all—reasonably priced.

"A commission of 2 or 3 percent is more than enough for a house that will sell itself," says Irving Price, a broker. It will help your bargaining position if you agree to make your house almost continuously available to potential buyers. And if you're moving within the same area, you can create a powerful case by telling the broker that you'll not only sell through him, you'll buy through him.

Don't spend a lot of time haggling, though. "All you should tell a broker," says one discounter, "is: 'Look, to sell my house, you won't have to do much work. If it were overpriced, it would be a different story. But this will sell itself.' If he won't cut his commission, there's another broker who will."

Dr. Zilavy can swear to that. When he was selling his Phoenix home, two brokers confided that they would accept commissions lower than 7 percent. One mentioned 6 percent, the other 5½ percent. And Dr. Zilavy wasn't trying to bargain anyone down.

CHAPTER

10 THE COMPLEAT GUIDE TO SELLING IT YOURSELF

As a ballpark estimate, it might take you 50 hours to sell your own home. If you are asking $200,000, you will save about $12,000 on the fee of a real-estate agent (assuming that he charged 6 percent). That amounts to $240 an hour. Nice work if you can get it.

Selling your own home can be not only profitable, but a snap. It's just not so torturous as some people would have you believe. One out of every 11 people, the estimate is, sells his home himself. This isn't surprising. When a house first goes on the market, it has the best chance of being sold. There's a backed-up pool of buyers, and they are especially interested in houses that are spanking fresh, houses that haven't sat for a while. And although many buyers are leery of a house "for sale by owner," others are under the impression that such houses are likely to be genuine bargains. (In my own experience, I must say, houses for sale by the owner tend to be grossly overpriced—either because the owners have inflated views of their homes' value or are just being greedy.)

Try selling your home by yourself for at least a month, and longer if yours is a nifty house in a posh neighborhood. If your attempt does not succeed, go with a broker. Brokers do have more potential buyers on tap, and they may succeed where you didn't.

THE RIGHT PRICE

Your first task is to establish a price. An easy way is to ask an experienced real-estate agent to do the job for you. Promise him that if you fall on your face trying to sell the house, you will give him the listing. Any reasonable agent will cooperate, and give you helpful advice to boot, such as information about the current mortgage situation in town.

Another tack is to hire a residential real-estate appraiser, as mentioned earlier. Appraisers tend to be conservative, so their estimates are usually on the low side. Call your local commercial bank or savings and loan association for names.

If you're willing to do some legwork, visit a local real-estate agency and ask to look through its book of houses that have sold recently—its "comparatives." Most agencies will oblige. By looking at the houses and adding and subtracting for features that your own house does or doesn't have, you can arrive at a sound estimate of your home's market value.

You could also telephone various real-estate agencies and ask to inspect various local houses for sale. If you don't sell your home yourself, you can use your experience with these agents to decide whom to list your house with. At the same time, ask any new neighbors what they paid for their homes, and compare their houses with yours. Use a comparison sheet like the one illustrated in Exhibit 10-1.

Once you have an estimate of what your house is worth, decide on a selling price. Remember: If your house is going for $200,000, you are saving a potential $12,000 real-estate agency fee. So keep your price reasonable. A 5 percent add-on to the market value, not the usual 10 percent, would be appropriate; the extra 5 percent is for bargaining, and just in case you have undervalued your house a bit.

Years ago, I was looking to buy a house in Passaic Park, N.J. A family friend was about to list his own house with a broker. I hurried over to inspect his house, then bid $72,000 for it. The owner ruminated and ruminated—and refused. Six months later, the poor fellow sold the house, through a broker, for exactly $72,000.

AVAILABLE FINANCING

Another task is to find out what financing you can arrange for a buyer. These days, attractive financing sells houses. Your mortgage contract will tell you whether the balance you owe—

COMPARING PROPERTIES

Address	Sale price	Asking price	Lot size	Rooms	Bedrooms	Baths	Age	Special features
Your house								

EXHIBIT 10-1

let's hope it's a lot—is assumable by a buyer, or whether the balance is due on sale. Even if the balance *is* due on sale, this provision may not be enforceable in the 14 states listed in Chapter 2. If the buyer can assume your mortgage, check whether you are off the hook as far as a prepayment penalty is concerned. When you speak to lenders, by the way, ask what financial information they would want from potential buyers.

If your mortgage isn't assumable, or if the balance you owe is so small that it doesn't matter, follow the procedures outlined in Chapter 2.

THE FACT SHEET

Good tidings about available financing should be a prominent feature of the fact sheet you write about your house. If your low-interest-rate mortgage balance can be assumed, for example, say so at the very top.

Fact sheets aren't common in many areas of the country, but they are a fine idea. Filling out a fact sheet will remind you of the virtues of your house and enable you to readily answer any buyer's questions. Give all visitors copies of your fact sheet, and mail copies to anyone who inquires about your house on the phone. A model fact sheet is illustrated in Exhibit 10-2.

THE HOUSE-FOR-SALE AD

Next, read through all your local newspapers to see where houses in your vicinity are being advertised. Place your ads in those papers. Sundays are the best days, and Saturdays are also good.

Don't be niggardly about the money you spend on advertising. One rule of thumb is that the cost of your ads should be 1 percent of your selling price. A generous advertising budget is vital in helping you sell your house yourself.

Try to have your ad stand out from the others. Consider buying a display ad, or one with extra white space or boldface type. Put a catchy headline on your ad, like EXECUTIVE HOUSE or MOVE-IN CONDITION. Or play up the chief virtue of your house—FIVE FIREPLACES, BATHROOM FOR EVERY BEDROOM, or whatever. If you're not inspired, or your house is just not inspirational, make it FOR SALE BY OWNER.

In the body of the ad, don't be flowery—be informative. Let your fact sheet guide you. Feature any favorable facts

EXHIBIT 10-2

MODEL FACT SHEET

Price: Style of house:

FOR SALE BY OWNER

Address:

Owner & phone numbers:

Directions:

Room sizes—Living room: Kitchen:
         Dining room: Family room:
         Master bedroom: Other bedrooms:

Bathrooms:

Garage:

Fireplace:

Patio:

Porch:

Closets:

Basement:

Heating:

Air-conditioning:

Insulation:

Disposal:

Appliances:

Age of house:

Personal property included/excluded:

Local schools—Public:
              Private:

Taxes:

Heating/cooling costs:

Possible financing:

Other information:

HOW TO BUY OR SELL YOUR HOME

about financing—"Assumable mortgage," for instance. Harp on any strong points your house has, such as a den next to the kitchen, a two-car attached garage, low heating bills. Try to discourage brokers with "principals only," though it won't do much good. Avd. annoy'g abbrvns. Don't say that your price is "negotiable," or that you are "asking" for such-and-such a price. But if your price is firm, say so.

Instead of just listing your phone number, consider announcing that you are having an open house, perhaps on both Saturday and Sunday, between designated hours. Some brokers claim that open houses don't do any good, but I have witnessed purchases during open houses.

Your ad should appear every weekend. If, after two weeks in a fairly active market, it hasn't pulled many callers, rewrite the ad. Here are fine examples of house-for-sale ads:

SANDS POINT, NEW YORK
"LAND'S END," 14 ACRES ON LONG ISLAND SOUND
Here is one of the great houses designed by Stanford White. It is on the tip of prestigious Sands Point, sheltered by 14 acres of huge trees. The 22-room residence has been scrupulously maintained and was recently updated to today's standards. The two-story entrance hall, the library, the living room, the dining room, and the morning room are all 30 feet or more in length. The master suite has twin dressing rooms and baths, plus a study; seven other bedrooms all have their own baths, and there are two bedrooms with baths and servants' quarters on the floor above. On the estate are a caretaker's cottage, a garage with two apartments, two greenhouses, and a new pool and pool house. There's also a tennis court and an orchard.
$2,500,000, Furnished

PACIFIC PALISADES
The home of President and Mrs. Reagan located in the Upper Riviera section of town. Secluded and peaceful, the residence has 11 rooms, with three bedrooms, three baths, and two servants' rooms and bath. Built 1956 as GE Showcase House, addition was made in 1961; painted and redecorated 1980. Swimming pool with deck. Extensive night lighting; magnificent views of Los Angeles, Santa Monica Bay by day, and a chain of lights known as the Queen's Necklace by night.
$1,900,000

PARADISE VALLEY, ARIZONA
A mansion on a mountain, this 36-room house stands on an equal number of acres atop Sugarloaf Mountain, with 360-degree views of the desert and valleys. With 14 bedrooms and 15 baths, the 31,000-square-foot house glories in such luxuries as inlaid walnut walls and doors, terrazzo flooring, and eight marble fireplaces imported from Portugal and Italy. There are decks on all three levels, and its spaces include a study and library, as well as a formal dining room. To delight the winter sports lover, there's an indoor ice-skating rink. There is also an Olympic-sized swimming pool....
$11,000,000

The above advertisements are genuine. They are marketed by Previews, an agency that specializes in unusual houses.

Incidentally, your house should have a "For Sale" sign, painted by a professional, on the lawn. But consider discouraging spur-of-the-moment visitors with "By appointment only." Those frantic efforts to straighten up can take any fun out of selling your home yourself.

DEALING WITH BUYERS

Memorize simple directions to your house. How many traffic lights from this block to that, landmarks where visitors should turn, and so forth. Have your fact sheet next to the phone. Schedule appointments 45 minutes apart; it should take 30 minutes for a buyer to inspect your house.

Ideally, the seller should be friendly but reserved. Don't show any avidity to sell your house. Don't be a high-pressure salesman constantly and shrilly pointing out this or that very small virtue. Tell yourself that the next person will buy, not this one.

In fact, as your buyers march through your house, point out any obvious drawbacks yourself, such as that the master bedroom has only one closet. It will help them trust you. But try to counter any flaws that you, or your visitors, mention—yes, the master bedroom has only one closet, but it's huge, or there are lots of other closets in other nearby rooms. Before your visitors leave, make sure they receive fact sheets.

Brokers are divided on whether buyers should be allowed to roam the house themselves or only with supervision. I prefer the owner to escort them, so that he can answer questions, counter any supposed defects the buyers mention, and offhandedly point out significant merits that might otherwise be missed, like the automatic air-filtration system.

EXHIBIT 10-3

BUYER QUALIFICATION FORM

Name: _____ Age: _____
Spouse: _____ Age: _____
Address: _____
Number of dependents: _____ Ages: _____ Phone: _____
Financing:
Preferred down payment: _____ Maximum: _____
Preferred monthly payment: _____ Maximum: _____

Husband	Wife
Employer: _____	Employer: _____
Address: _____	Address: _____
Position: _____	Position: _____
Length of service: _____	Length of service: _____
Monthly income: _____	Monthly income: _____

Family earnings for past 3 years:
19____ $_____ ; 19____ $_____ ; 19____ $_____

	Monthly	Yearly
Husband's income:	$_____	$_____
Other income:	_____	_____
Wife's income:	_____	_____
Other income:	_____	_____
Totals:	_____	_____

Assets		Liabilities		
			Monthly payment	Unpaid balance
Cash: _____		Auto: _____	$_____	$_____
Stocks, bonds, etc.: _____		Real estate: ____	_____	_____
Real estate: _____		Loans: _____	_____	_____
Other: _____		Other: _____	_____	_____
Total: _____		Total: _____	_____	_____

Have you had any credit problems during the past 10 years?
Yes _____ No _____
Date: _____ Signatures of buyers: _____

What if you have had plenty of visitors but no nibbles after a few weeks? Since you don't have an agent to give you advice, call upon a friend. The friend should inspect your house inside and out, and give you a frank appraisal. Judith Nelson, the wife of a psychiatrist in New Jersey, sold her house herself, and when a neighbor was having trouble going the same route, volunteered to help. The problem, she decided, was that the house lacked sex appeal. Her recommended solution: $300 worth of house plants, including such unusual varieties as dracaena and bromeliad.

QUALIFYING BUYERS
The time to start qualifying a buyer—finding out whether he can actually afford your house—is when he makes a "closing" comment. Such as: "Would you take $180,000 for this house?" or "When can the buyers move in?" or "Do the carpets and drapes go with the house?" (The best response to "Would you take $180,000 for this house?" is "Let's talk about it." Sit down with your quarry and explain how you came up with the price. If you would actually consider $180,000, you might counter with, "Would you put that offer in writing?")

To qualify a buyer, explain that by not using a broker you can sell your house more reasonably, but you have to do the agent's job of making sure that any interested party can afford it. You therefore have to find out whether a potential buyer's gross monthly income, minus other long-term expenses, is three times the monthly housing payment. You also need to know how long the buyer has been employed at one place, what assets he has, and so forth. Have the buyer fill out and sign a form like the one illustrated in Exhibit 10-3.

Your next step is to joyfully take your ready, willing, and able buyer to your lawyer's office to sign the contract.

CHAPTER

11 *THE HARD-TO-SELL HOUSE*

I have good news for you. Only seldom does it happen that someone is so stymied in selling a house that he has to tear it down and sell only the land. Or that, bloodied and beaten, he winds up donating the place to a local chapter of Goodwill Industries. In fact, I have never heard of such a case—or even of an instance where a person of (say) age 25 tried unsuccessfully to sell a house and was constrained to stay there until he died at (say) 76, leaving the accursed place to unappreciative heirs. Most houses, in short, get sold.

The most common cause of difficulty, of course, is an inflated price. Once you cut the price, the house is almost as fresh as one newly placed on the market, and it should attract a lot of new lookers (for whom your high-priced house was just out of range) as well as some old lookers. If you can't bring yourself to cut the price quite yet, give yourself a deadline: Either your house sells in two months, or you reduce the price.

If you're sure that your house isn't overpriced, it's a different story. Your task is to find out why it's taking you longer to sell than it's taking other people. A broker in Hohokus, N.J., John Faulkner, points out that "there's always a reason a house is hard to sell. And there's always a way to rectify a problem."

Begin by taking relatively minor steps. Change the ads that have been running, or change the publications in which you have been advertising. If your agency has been running ads, start running different ones of your own.

If your agent seems to have been slothful and your contract has quite a while to run, ask your lawyer about firing the agent for cause and signing up with someone more energetic. Or lower the price and try to sell the house on your own.

If available money seems to have been the sticking-point, consider helping buyers with a little financing. But, as you were warned earlier, be careful.

Perhaps your house is just undistinguished, unmemorable. Besides buying plants, you might spend a few hundred on a dazzling chandelier, or an imposing front door with colored glass. You might remove old carpeting and have the floors scraped. Somehow, give the place some sex appeal.

I was once selling a house that had fading wallpaper and peeling paint throughout. Rather than spruce the place up, I deducted something from the selling price—to let the new owners decorate the place to their individual taste. Alas, fading wallpaper and peeling paint drive all customers away. I wound up repapering and repainting with bland but not unattractive designs and colors—and quickly selling the house.

If there is something glaringly wrong with your house, have the defect fixed, spending the minimum. I once saw a house, overlooking a brook, the rear yard of which had been blacktopped. Evidently the owner couldn't abide mowing the grass. Naturally, no one would buy such a strange place. I don't know what the owner finally did, but he would have been wise to pay to have the blacktop removed and sod installed. (A shrewd buyer would have bid a shamelessly low price, calculating in the cost of restoring the yard.)

Paying for a major improvement—say, a remodeled kitchen—is a dangerous gamble. It's highly unlikely that you will get the full cost back, and your house *still* might not sell. If you are sure that your kitchen is badly outdated (buyers see it and flee in horror), do the minimum. Install new Formica cabinets, say, but don't go the whole route of installing new appliances, a new ceiling, a new floor, and so on.

If you're a doctor, lawyer, architect, or whatever, and your house has offices, lots of luck. Home-offices have been fading away, partly because many communities ban them. (In residential districts, says John Faulkner, they have an aura of commercialism.) You are going to have to market your home energetically, calling local hospitals, law firms, architectural firms, looking for professionals who might be interested. You would also do well to advertise in specialty journals.

Above all, don't panic if your property isn't selling. If you want to move into another house you have purchased, you can always rent your old house temporarily. After all, the solution to your problem may just be a matter of more time.

THE MARKETING MAVENS
Three reasons that many houses don't sell readily is that they are (1) very expensive for their area, (2) very expensive for any area, or (3) unusual. If that's your own problem, consider signing aboard with a company that specializes in selling such houses. Two excellent companies are Sotheby Parke Bernet International Realty Corporation in New York City and Previews in Greenwich, Conn. Both specialize in the unusual and the unusually expensive. And there is not an iota of love lost between them. The two companies harbor toward each other the same feelings that Yankee fans and Red Sox fans have for each other.

Just because a house is expensive doesn't make it a candidate for Previews or Sotheby. As Bruce Wennerstrom, the charming, intelligent president of Previews, reports, a $600,000 house will be a cinch for anyone to sell—if it's in Greenwich or Beverly Hills. And as Charles H. Seilheimer Jr., the charming, intelligent president of Sotheby, reports, a $250,000 house in Palm Beach isn't appropriate for his agency—unless it has two swimming pools, six fireplaces, a Jacuzzi, and just one bedroom. Houses that *are* suitable need a wide market—and will interest buyers living quite a distance away.

Very expensive or very unusual houses need a wide market because potential buyers constitute a small slice of the population. In 1980, reports Wennerstrom, there were 2,780,000 residential properties sold retail, and 98.7 percent sold for under $250,000. So the pool of prospects for a $250,000+ house is a tiny 1.3 percent of the populace. And when someone has a property worth $1 million, probably less than 0.1 percent can afford it. A buyer probably isn't going to be living up the road. He might be living in Saudi Arabia. Or, as Seilheimer says, "You sell luxury property like a fine painting. If you have a Picasso to sell, you don't go to your local art shop."

But even relatively cheap houses may be suitable for Sotheby or Previews if they are special enough. Sotheby sold the house shown in Andrew Wyeth's painting, "Christina's World," for less than $100,000. And Seilheimer says that he would be happy to sell a house worth a mere $50,000 "if it had once been Betsy Ross's bungalow."

Wennerstrom recalls selling a $60,000 house in Maine: "It had been built by a couple who were looking for privacy and seclusion, so they built their home in the woods, with nobody for miles and miles around. When it came time to sell, there were no buyers for miles and miles, either. It was a matter of finding somebody seeking the same kind of seclusion."

By and large, the least expensive houses sold by Previews and Sotheby cost $250,000. The *typical* property the two agencies sell is worth around a million. Previews is selling one for $8 million now (owned by a rock impresario) and Sotheby is selling one for $20 million (owned by a Chrysler heiress).

NUTS AND BOLTS

As a commission, Previews charges 11 percent, 5 percent going to the participating broker. Sotheby charges 10 percent, with 5 percent for the broker. Both companies levy an up-front charge, usually 1 or 2 percent of the selling price. It's for advertising, for using mailing lists, and such. There's a sliding scale: The more expensive the property, the less the percentage. The up-front charge is credited against the final fee if the property is sold, and most properties do get sold.

The luxury-house market has only slightly reflected the sluggishness the ordinary real-estate market has suffered in recent years. One reason is that creative financing has always been prevalent in the luxury-house field. As Seilheimer puts it, "Even the rich don't usually have $5 million in their checking accounts." So high-interest mortgages, or nonexistent mortgages, haven't mattered much.

Sotheby's listing agreement runs two years, Previews' three. Sometimes it does take a while to sell a luxury house, simply because of the months it takes to get ads in major magazines, and the months it takes to get rich European lounge lizards to visit this country. Both Sotheby and Previews use exclusive right-to-sell contracts. If you sell the house yourself while it's listed, you still owe a commission. Both companies will estimate the market value of your property.

A GHOST-FREE HOUSE

Sotheby and Previews have elaborate and imaginative marketing strategies.

Previews has its own offices in major U.S. cities, along with a network of 15,000 brokers here and abroad, who receive color brochures of properties for sale and a color catalogue six times a year. All of the residential properties are shown in its bimonthly magazine, *Homes International,* which circulates (among other places) to passengers on 16 major airlines. Previews also publishes an annual catalogue, distributed in 50 countries and updated with supplements every other month. Important customers receive videotapes of major properties.

It also engages in lots of sophisticated direct-mail campaigns. To sell a house in Florida that could accommodate an 85-foot yacht, Previews used a list of the names of everyone

EXHIBIT 11-1

GIMMICKS, UNLIMITED

To unload hard-to-sell houses, people have turned not only to creative financing but also to creative selling. The legality of any of these methods may vary according to state or locality. Check with a lawyer first.

- The Middleton family of Illinois promised that whoever bought their house would win a trip to Hawaii. They sold their house.
- The Cisneys of Wisconsin gave their farmhouse to the person who wrote the best conclusion to this sentence: "I want to own a farmhouse in Wisconsin because. . . ." Contestants paid $50 apiece to enter, and the Cisneys limited entries to 3,500. In effect, the sale price was $175,000.
- To sell the houses of workers it was relocating, General Motors put new cars in the garages.
- A family in California, like many others, put their house on the auction block. Winning bid: $1.6 million.
- The Redmans of Virginia sold raffle tickets for their house at $100 each. Part of the profits went to a local Boys Club. The Redmans wound up with $133,000, and the Boys Club made a handsome profit. Others have tried this technique, too. But it is of doubtful legality.

HOW TO BUY OR SELL YOUR HOME

who had purchased a yacht 40 feet or longer since 1960. To sell a house in Escondido, Calif., with a 20-car garage, Previews is using lists of recent purchasers of Rolls-Royces, Ferraris, Aston Martins, and Mercedes-Benz 450 SLs. To sell a game preserve outside of Johannesburg, Previews compiled a list of big-game hunters (and sold the property to two San Franciscans who had never been hunting in their lives).

Previews, incidentally, has peddled four of Dean Martin's houses, Julie Andrews' house, Kim Novak's house, Jimmy Stewart's ranch, Gerald Ford's house, the Kennedy estate in Virginia, and Ronald Reagan's house.

One of the most interesting properties Previews has sold was a house built in New Jersey in Colonial times by a man named Jamie Dawes. Dawes was terrified of ghosts. Ghosts, as everyone knew then (but as we seem to have forgotten), hide in corners. So Dawes' house was built with no corners. Everything was round. When Previews sold the place, it came with a document certifying that the house was ghost-free.

Sotheby engages in the same sort of sophisticated marketing strategy. It employs a select list of 400 brokers in affluent communities around the country, as well as 50 or so brokers abroad, and has a half-dozen of its own broker agencies in major cities.

It regularly sends color brochures describing its properties to these brokers and to 4,000 well-to-do people "who know what Sotheby Parke Bernet is all about," including plantation owners in South Carolina and Georgia, members of ritzy country clubs, and so forth. Sotheby's corporate newsletter, printed 10 times a year, has a real-estate section, and goes to 100,000 people. Its annual book of properties is called *Unique Homes*.

Sotheby has sold property for Henry Ford II, Steve Martin, Richard M. Nixon, and Otto Preminger. It handled the most expensive single-user residential property ever sold in America. Price: $14.5 million. Seller: film producer Dino DeLaurentiis. Buyer: country-Western singer Kenny Rogers.

Every month Sotheby advertises in hundreds of magazines. Is its chief magazine *The New Yorker? Connoisseur? Medical Economics?* Heck, no. It might be *Ducks Unlimited*—a superb medium to sell luxury houses in the duck-hunting areas of east Maryland and South Carolina. Incidentally, Seilheimer reports that the single area of the country with the most luxury properties is Manhattan.

BUYING

CHAPTER

12 *THE BEST CITIES TO LIVE IN – AND THE WORST*

Not to keep you in suspense, the best American city to live in is San Diego. The worst: Detroit. And in general, the future of American cities is rosy.

These are some of the findings of a Delphi poll among 47 noted authorities that Elizabeth Horton of *Science Digest* magazine and I conducted recently. In a typical Delphi poll, a group of experts are asked the same or similar questions at least twice. Their answers usually change somewhat in subsequent rounds, once they have learned the names of their colleagues and the consensus from the first balloting. Presumably, the experts cling to the answers they are sure of and join the majority where they are unsure, so that the final consensus represents the firmest views of the entire group. As a forecasting tool, the Delphi poll has repeatedly proved itself extraordinarily accurate.

The Delphi questionnaire on cities was devised with the help of Kristina Ford, assistant professor at the Graduate School of Public Administration at New York University; George Sternlieb, director of the Rutgers Center for Urban Policy Research; Dean L. Macris, planning director for San Francisco; Marjorie Macris, planning director for Marin County, Calif.; and Murray Turoff, an authority on Delphi polls.

CITIES OF GOLD, CITIES OF DROSS

The panelists—who included city planners, architects, and university professors—were asked to rank 55 of the largest cities in the country on a number of touchstones, including their prospects, management, attractiveness, employment picture, business climate, and so forth. They were also free to comment on cities not among the 55.

The Cities of Gold proved to be San Diego, Portland (Ore.), Seattle, Minneapolis, and Albuquerque.

The Cities of Dross were Detroit, Dayton, Buffalo, Akron, Newark, Cleveland, and Birmingham.

A few cities—New York and Chicago among them—received strangely mixed notices from the panelists.

As for big cities in general, instead of sinking into a slough of fiscal horror, physical decay, unemployment, racial enmity, and crime, most are in for a healthy and prosperous time. This optimistic prediction even applies to the majority of older cities in the East and Midwest, cities widely regarded as beyond salvation. The average American city will not only endure, but will thrive.

Clear evidence of the panelists' optimism about American cities came when they rated the prospects of the largest cities in the country. Only five cities, the panel concluded, will decline; 27 will hold their own; 23 will do better. The average city among the 55 wound up neatly poised between the "hold its own" and the "do better" categories.

CAUSES FOR CHEER

Why this optimism? Because the cost of energy may drive people back to the cities, the panelists thought, and the Baby Bust may remove the magnet that attracted them to the suburbs in the first place.

"The energy crisis has been a blessing in disguise," says Gloria S. McGregor, an executive with the Morrison-Knudson Company in San Francisco. "Fifteen years ago, if you wanted a bigger house, you just moved to the suburbs—because you had cheap energy. But now it costs a lot more to build a new house than to remodel an old one, so people are staying put." Then, too, with family size dwindling, the bloom is rubbing off suburban life. Says McGregor, "Today, people are not so seduced by the prospect of a little half-acre in the country with room for the kids and dogs."

THE BEST CITIES TO LIVE IN—AND THE WORST

EXHIBIT 12-1

WHICH CITIES WILL FLOURISH? WHICH WILL FOUNDER?

The Delphi panelists were asked to rank 55 of the largest cities in the country, paying keenest attention to each city's employment picture, its attractiveness for business, its fiscal health, and its political leadership. Here is how the cities ranked, from best to worst:

These will do better:

San Diego	Salt Lake City
Portland, Ore.	Boston
Seattle	Phoenix
Minneapolis	Houston
Albuquerque	Baltimore
Dallas	Honolulu
Denver	Atlanta
San Antonio	Kansas City, Mo.
San Francisco	Oklahoma City
San Jose	Tampa
Sacramento	Tulsa
Tucson	

These will hold their own:

Fort Lauderdale	Pittsburgh
Washington	Louisville
Milwaukee	Columbus, Ohio
Chicago	Los Angeles
New York	New Orleans
Riverside	Indianapolis
Richmond, Va.	Philadelphia
Cincinnati	Miami
El Paso	Memphis
Omaha	Rochester
Jacksonville	St. Louis
Nashville	Birmingham
Anaheim	Cleveland
Hartford	

These will slip:

Newark	Dayton
Akron	Detroit
Buffalo	

Besides, influential citizens are becoming concerned, and as a result of their efforts, many of our wilting cities are beginning to flower. "I'm very encouraged," says Richard F. Babcock, a Chicago lawyer who specializes in urban law. "I think more corporation men are beginning to say, 'We can't just live out here in Lake Forest and commute in on a train to Standard Oil. We've got to get involved in the city.'"

FROST BELT VERSUS SUN BELT

People who feel gloomy about the state of American cities are usually thinking of the Frost Belt. And most of the panelists did agree that while cities in the Sun Belt will thrive, those in the Frost Belt will manage only to hold their own.

"I certainly believe that many cities in the Northeast and the Midwest are still looking for the bottom," says Paul R. Dommel, a senior fellow at the Brookings Institution in Washington, D.C. "A lot of these cities are bleeding economically. Reindustrialization is too late for them. The jobs have already gone, and no wonder. You have lower labor costs in the South. A businessman will have a helluva lot less hassle with the zoning, with the environmental regulations, with all kinds of things than he would in the North."

An eloquent minority of the panelists, though, felt that not only will the Frost Belt outshine the Sun Belt, but that the Sun Belt is in for a nightmarish time.

Boosters of the Frost Belt point to the imaginative rebuilding of such cities as Baltimore and Boston, to new high-technology and information industries making their homes in Northern cities, to the fact that the Frost Belt cities already have their infrastructures (streets, sewers, and such) in place, whereas it will be extraordinarily expensive for the spreading Sun Belt cities to build new infrastructures. Says Calvin L. Beale, leader of the population studies group for the Department of Agriculture, "For most of the Northern cities, even Newark, I think the worst has passed."

The Sun Belt cities, moreover, may face problems of overcrowding, pollution, inadequate transportation, unbalanced budgets, unemployment, energy shortages, and social conflict.

"I have a feeling," says Michael P. Brooks, dean of the College of Design at Iowa State University, "that some of the Sun Belt cities have enjoyed—I was going to say 'their day in the sun,' but that would be too terrible a pun. Cities in the

Southwest in particular are going to be crammed with people. And they seem to be dominated by the spirit of J.R. Ewing. A 'Don't bother us, we're okay' spirit. As a result, they are not going to attack their problems very seriously. What I expect is an awful lot of urban sprawl, smog, and so on. I'm more optimistic about cities in the Northeast and Midwest facing up to their problems."

Daniel Lauber, president of Planning/Communications in Evanston, Ill., feels Southern workers will "eventually realize they're underpaid. There are going to be dozens of Norma Raes organizing unions, and wages are going to shoot up."

Says Margery alChalabi, vice president of the Real Estate Research Corporation in Chicago, "It takes more energy to air-condition facilities than to heat them, and Houston and Dallas are both dependent on air-conditioning for a large portion of the year. They are in jeopardy not only from energy costs but from overtaxing their infrastructures. The growing division between the well-to-do and the poorer neighborhoods is going to cause social friction."

A significant change between the voting on the first Delphi questionnaire and the second was that the panelists became more optimistic about the Frost Belt cities and less optimistic about their counterparts in the Sun Belt.

THE EDEN OF CITIES

Still, when the cities were ranked according to their prospects, Sun Belt cities were sprinkled near the top; Frost Belt cities hogged the bottom. If there was one overall winner, it was *San Diego*. It topped the list of cities with good prospects and of those best to retire to; it was near the top among best-managed cities and cities most attractive for their size.

Panelists praised San Diego for its climate, its cultural and recreational activities, its economy, its government, its housing, its physical setting. "It's a kind of Los Angeles without the problems of Los Angeles," says Larry Reich, director of city planning for Baltimore. "It probably comes closest among the major cities to being Edenlike."

But one panelist even criticized Eden. "San Diego just doesn't have the home industries that Minneapolis has," says Babcock. "It is the only city of its size that I know of that doesn't have a bank with a billion dollars worth of assets—there just isn't all that much industry there."

Tied for second place among cities with good prospects were Portland and Seattle. *Portland* was also close to the top of the list among trend-setting cities, best-managed cities, and best cities to retire to; it was the most attractive city in its size category.

Among the reasons panelists praised Portland: its local government's concern about neighborhoods, the high priority given to the environment, its diversity, its high employment level, its progressive government, and its cultural advantages. "It's a city that has its act together," says McGregor. "If you don't mind the rain and the drizzle," says Babcock, "it's just one hell of an attractive city." The only demur comes from Rick Wiederhorn, senior planner for St. Paul, who claims that Portland only emulates what other cities have done, "but does an excellent job of tooting its own horn."

Seattle was a runner-up among best cities to retire to, best-managed cities, and trend-setting cities. It tied San Francisco for the lead in attractiveness for its size. Seattle's virtues include good government, a revitalized downtown area, strong inner-city neighborhoods, excellent recreational facilities, good mass transit, and an impressive setting.

EDEN NORTH

Minneapolis rivaled San Diego in its performance in the poll. Ranking just below Portland and Seattle in its prospects, Minneapolis was also the best-managed city and the leading trendsetter, as well as a runner-up for attractiveness for its size, for the most underrated city, and for best city to retire to.

Minneapolis was praised for its financial expertise (property taxes have been cut for several years running), its healthy residential neighborhoods, its parks and cultural facilities, its system of sidewalks (called skyways) enclosed within buildings in the downtown area, its comprehensive planning, and its vitality. Jane Holtz Kay of Boston, an architecture critic, says that Minneapolis "has been on the cutting edge of reform for a century, and still is." Says McGregor, "People there are strong physically and mentally—I guess they have to be, to survive that climate. It's a city that makes you feel it's bustling all the time. I was probably more stimulated, and had more friends there, than any other place I've lived—and I've lived in quite a number. In the end, though, the climate got me down, so that's a minus for sure."

The four cities at the bottom of the list were Akron, Buffalo, Dayton, and Detroit, all industrial cities on the decline. About *Akron* and *Dayton,* Wiederhorn says, "Some cities in Ohio just don't seem to have made the effort that other communities in similar situations have." *Buffalo,* according to Kristina Ford, "has a higher percentage of gray days than any other city in America." And of *Detroit,* Brooks says: "The Renaissance Center is an example of how *not* to conduct a major inner-city development. They've simply created a fortress surrounded by a wasteland and not made any concentrated effort to develop the city as a whole. Detroit remains a fairly unpleasant place to go." Says Babcock, "I'm not sure that the automobile manufacturers are all that smart, and I think it's going to take them a lot longer than they think to bounce back."

UNDERRATED CITIES
Cincinnati was considered the most underrated city, and one of the best-managed. (Cincinnati and Milwaukee, says Babcock, "are *notorious* for being well run.") Panelists spoke of Cincinnati's ethnic diversity, its cultural life, its location on the Ohio River, its form of government (it's one of the largest cities with a city manager), its "aliveness." Other underrated cities included Baltimore, Kansas City, and Pittsburgh.

Baltimore is the model success story. "It was in the pits 20 years ago," says Larry Reich. "Even lower than Cleveland. Now the downtown has been turned around completely; the waterfront, which was a real mess, is a pleasant place with a shopping center and nice restaurants." He attributes the city's ability to lift itself up in great part to an alliance between the public and private sectors.

Kansas City, says Rex R. Campbell, professor of sociology at the University of Missouri, has a solid, diverse economy and a relatively mild climate.

Pittsburgh has diversified industry, a sense of neighborhood, and a well-educated work force. "Culturally and intellectually, Pittsburgh is a city that has been alive and remains alive," says David A. Caputo of the political-science department of Purdue University.

SOUTHERN TIME BOMBS
Overrated cities included Houston and Dallas (tied), Los Angeles, Phoenix, New Orleans, Atlanta, and Miami.

"*Houston*'s lack of zoning and planning are time bombs that are ticking away," says James V. Cunningham, professor of social work at the University of Pittsburgh. Says Dommel, "It has a *mammoth* section of poverty. The highway system is so poor that the traffic jams at rush hour are horrendous, and I've read that there have been shootings when people were caught in those lines." Wiederhorn doesn't think that "people in Houston or Dallas have any real grasp of the implications of wild growth at any cost."

Kristina Ford calls *Dallas* "an undifferentiated plain—one monotonous idea." Says Beale, "You have a tremendously built-up area, and around it are just freeways and desolation." Niles Hansen of the University of Texas at Austin, commenting on the fact that Dallas is in the middle of nowhere, says, "Goodness knows why it's there, in more ways than one."

Los Angeles seems to be the city people love to hate. "The smog was so oppressive, I couldn't wait to get out," says Beale.

"It's an inhabited ruin. The quality of life is absolutely abysmal. The freeway system is so clogged that trying to get from here to there is murder," says McGregor. "It has no character, no center."

Phoenix, says Brooks, "strikes me as a Los Angeles of the future. Development is occurring there relatively untrammeled by planning and zoning."

New Orleans, according to the panelists, is deteriorating. "They've got about all the mileage they can get out of the French Quarter," says Brooks.

Atlanta is burdened with a high crime rate; its attempts to rehabilitate its older areas have not been uniformly successful. "Underground Atlanta," says Babcock, "is a junk heap."

Gloria McGregor thinks that "in many areas, *Miami* is a grungy city. And for many years it's been a haven for the criminal element, attracted to the wealth there. It's a tough place to live in—anything can happen."

OF MAYORS AND THINGS

Among the cities considered best-managed were Milwaukee and Chicago—though some panelists thought Chicago was also *poorly* managed.

Milwaukee is "one of those sleeper towns," says Wiederhorn. "It's vibrant." Others talked of its low crime rate, its beautiful setting, its exciting downtown area, its pride. But above all they laud its government: "Milwaukee," says Babcock, "once had a socialist mayor for what seemed a hundred years, and he was the most frightening capitalist you could imagine."

Chicago was praised and panned in almost equal numbers. It was voted the most attractive city with a population over two million—and was a runner-up among *least* attractive cities with populations over two million. It was also rated a city that would surprise people with its strengths—and (with fewer votes) a city that would surprise people with its weaknesses.

"A lot of controversy goes on there of a stimulating nature," says Cunningham. Babcock calls Chicago "a healthy, vigorous city." Critics zeroed in on Chicago's poverty ("If you're black," says Lauber, "Chicago stinks.") and its political deterioration. "It's probably the one big city in the country that has a planning department more impotent than a eunuch," Lauber says.

Cleveland and New York were among the worst-managed cities. *"Cleveland,"* according to Cunningham, "has a long history of mayors who were either embroiled in controversy or incompetent."

New York was rated a poorly managed city, but it was also a city that would surprise people with its strengths, an overrated city, a trend-setter, one of the most attractive cities with populations over two million, and one of the most unattractive.

Critics, like Brooks, say that New York is "too expensive, too rude. To some extent, it personifies all of the traits of rampant urbanism." McGregor says that "many of the institutions are very crooked, and bribery is a way of life there." "I was in and out of the city five or six times recently," says Caputo, "and every time I went it seemed to have deteriorated further."

Big Apple polishers included Niles Hansen: "Everybody always says, 'Well, New York is played out, everybody's leaving,' and so forth. It's true that just about every major employment activity that New York has invented eventually leaves for cheaper labor elsewhere. But New York always reinvents something else." To Kristina Ford, New York is "the most diverse city in the world. And you feel that what's going on here really matters."

Asked about the up-and-down ratings of New York, Mayor Edward I. Koch told me, "People have always had a love-hate relationship with this city, but right now it's mostly love."

Boston led the list of cities that would surprise people with their strengths. Its successful downtown remodeling is often likened to Baltimore's. Jane Holtz Kay calls it a city of the future, with its emphasis on walking, row houses, energy-saving.

ALL IN APPEARANCES

Among the cities rated the most attractive to live in during the years to come were Madison, Santa Fe, and San Francisco.

Madison was praised for its attractive setting, its recreational opportunities, the high educational level of the population, its excellent government.

Santa Fe won plaudits for "its respect for its historic roots," as Cunningham put it. "It has preserved itself in a very authentic way."

San Francisco was complimented on a number of counts, from its educational institutions to its public transportation.

EXHIBIT 12-2

BEST-MANAGED, WORST-MANAGED, AND SURPRISING CITIES

According to the Delphi poll, the best-managed cities are:

Minneapolis	Portland, Ore.
Seattle	Baltimore
Milwaukee	Chicago
Cincinnati	San Diego

The worst-managed cities:

Cleveland	Houston
Chicago	Boston
New York	Detroit

Cities surprising for their strengths:

Boston	Chicago
Baltimore	Milwaukee
New York	Pittsburgh

Cities surprising for their weaknesses:

Houston	Chicago
Atlanta	Detroit
Phoenix	Miami
Los Angeles	

McGregor says that San Francisco "gives you all kinds of opportunities to do whatever it turns you on to do." And Babcock captured the essence of San Francisco in a word: "cute."

The least attractive cities to live in during the years to come included *Gary* and *Scranton,* two cities in which, according to Hansen, "everything is grimy." In Gary, says Caputo, "Racial animosity is a key problem. So many things have gone wrong, it would be very difficult at this point to turn it around."

SAN DIEGO VERSUS DETROIT

A fascinating question, relating to all these ratings of American cities, is: Why are San Diego, Portland, and Seattle so blessed by good fortune? What differentiates them from accursed places like Detroit? Why do certain cities seem destined to thrive, others to decay?

Size, in the opinion of most panelists, doesn't really matter—so long as a city is not *too* big. The median ideal city size chosen was 230,000, but generally the experts pooh-poohed the significance of mere numbers. "I don't think there's an optimal size," says Babcock. "I can like Chicago, and I can like a tiny town in Montana." Says Dommel, "I don't think size is crucial. Akron and Fort Lauderdale are in approximately the same size category, but for God's sake, it's a lot easier to manage Fort Lauderdale." To Gloria McGregor, "a lot has to do with the way a city is planned. If it's an amorphous blob, even 250,000 is hard to deal with."

Yet cities as large as New York, the panelists felt, may have special problems. With New York, Chicago, and Los Angeles in mind, Larry Reich says, "I think that when a city gets to be over four million, it's very difficult to handle." Margery alChalabi agrees, but she notes that "while New York is not very manageable, you need that concentration to have the diversity available only in New York City or a place that size. There is probably an optimum size for *running* a city, but I'm not sure there's an optimum size for needing it to exist."

In the first round of the poll, not a single panelist voted for "homogeneity of social and economic classes" as a factor influencing the future of a city. It was dropped from the second questionnaire. But in later interviews, the panelists seemed to think that homogeneity is a wonderfully desirable factor—but by "homogeneity" they meant, of course, not a sameness of impoverished people but a sameness of the well-to-do.

"One of the reasons why the Twin Cities are so successful," says Wiederhorn, "is that we have a small minority population. The more heterogeneous the society, the more the potential for conflict and strife. I'm not saying that's good or bad—it's just a comment. That's why I see the potential for social strife in cities like Miami and Houston increasing enormously."

Calvin Beale is equally frank: "It's practically impossible for a city or a metropolitan area to have a comparatively high percentage of blacks or Chicanos or Puerto Ricans without having a lot of conflict, without white flight to the suburbs, and without a fairly high level of social disorganization on such important indexes as crime and drug use."

But, at the core, what distinguishes cities with a future from cities with no future is jobs. The Delphi panelists voted "employment picture" and "attractiveness for business" number one and number two among the factors that determine whether a city will flourish. And certainly the cities that are being rejuvenated, and those cities that were never senescent at all, are blessed with business communities that are proud of and loyal to their cities, and with political leadership and a business sector that work together smoothly.

"I think there are movers and shakers in Philadelphia, Boston, and Minneapolis who just aren't going to allow their cities to go down beyond a certain point," says Babcock. "And I'm not sure you'll find that in Phoenix, Houston, or Los Angeles. The Medicis of the last half of the 20th century in our country are the businessmen who take pride in their cities."

CHAPTER

13 EVERYONE'S DREAM: THE CUSTOM-BUILT HOUSE

Herewith . . . tales of screaming terror, certain to make your skin crawl, your hair stand up straight, your blood run cold. They are best read on a bone-chilling night inside a gloomy country home miles and miles from its nearest neighbor, with the wind howling outside . . .

When he decided to build a new house, Lowell H. Hansen, a Denver radiologist, chose as his architect "a glib talker who impressed us with his progressive and unusual ideas." His 14 years of training, the architect boasted, included time spent under Frank Lloyd Wright. The Hansens later learned that the training consisted of a one-week seminar.

The architect gave the builders (general contractors) only a few days to submit bids. One builder's bid came in 50 percent above the estimate. A second builder simply refused to bid, given the short time. The bid of a third builder was only $4,500 above the estimate, and was victorious. Sometime later, the Hansens learned that the architect had created and sold the third builder's company, and had probably assisted in preparing its bid.

A good engineer the architect was not. "Workmen were at the house almost every week, correcting and recorrecting goofs," says Dr. Hansen. "In the end, I counted no less than

65 separate mistakes that were made." A toilet flushed steaming hot water. A rock wall had so many minute openings that the wind came through in 30 places, by actual count. And during a good downpour, "water poured in through the cracks in the window frames, down the flues, through the basement windows, through the stone floor on the porch into the basement ceiling and out the heating vents, into the inside walls, through the ceiling electrical fixtures, and, of course, through the 30 places in the rock wall."

The Hansens eventually won a fat judgment against the architect, who countered brilliantly by declaring bankruptcy. "We finally sold the house for the mortgage balance," says Dr. Hansen, "and today we are still feeling the financial pinch from the disaster."

A Pennsylvania doctor, Sol Browdy, chose an architect with a reputation for fine contemporary designs. Although the Browdys wanted a Colonial, the architect was determined on a ranch, "come hell or high costs." In fact, he resolutely insisted on designs that were Byzantine in their complexity.

When they opened the bids from four builders, says the doctor, it was "one of the saddest moments of our lives." The lowest bid was for 50 percent more than they were willing to spend. "So, with heavy hearts, my wife and I decided to commit home-icide."

Later, the architect had the effrontery to submit a bill for a commission based *not* on the targeted price of the house but on the lowest actual bid. And a general practitioner whom Dr. Browdy ran into told him that the architect had done the same thing to him *twice*—"He had drawn up overpriced plans and charged on the basis of the lowest bid."

Masroor Ali, a general surgeon in Michigan, chose a builder who came recommended by the doctor's friends. The builder's estimated price for a house was $104,000, not including $28,000 for land. After receiving $60,000, Dr. Ali reports, the builder simply disappeared—"I never saw him again." The house, at that point, was only a shell. And no other builders Dr. Ali approached were willing to complete the job, since they didn't want to be responsible for the work already done. So he wound up finishing the house with his own hands. It took him two back-breaking years.

EVERYONE'S DREAM: THE CUSTOM-BUILT HOUSE

Emanuel Klein, a family physician in Bloomington, Ind., bought a new house where his wife, a psychiatrist, could meet patients. The builder came highly recommended, and "it may sound silly, but he had clean fingernails."

They went ahead without an architect, and agreed to do some of the simpler work themselves to save money—"the sorriest decision we ever made." The work they were called upon to do was both tedious and laborious. "Unless you're a real handyman type with a lot of spare time," Dr. Klein warns, "don't you do it, either."

As the doctor recalls, fiasco followed fiasco. The roof and the foundation leaked. The heating-cooling system neither heated nor cooled. The carport slab began to crack. The electrical contractor kept walking off the job.

At the doctor's request, another builder examined the house and "found an awesome number of defects we had missed," from inadequate insulation to a bad painting job.

As the finishing touch, the builder brought suit against the Kleins for $25,000 they supposedly owed. (He didn't win.)

A pediatrician in Maryland, Andrew G. Aronfy, wanted a new home-office. He, too, bypassed an architect and hired a builder directly. A month after the doctor moved in, the builder went broke and skipped. All sorts of odds and ends went uncompleted, including the installation of storm windows and screens. The drain in the utility room backed up, ruining records, supplies, and equipment. When it rained, water seeped under the doctor's waiting-room door.

Like being knighted or winning the Nobel Prize, you know you have arrived when you can afford to build your own house. Anything you have ever dreamed about—a private study, a library, a fireplace in the bathroom—can now be yours.

Perhaps it's their high hopes, their dreamy self-satisfaction, that help explain why so many people emerge from the experience filled with bitterness. Another possible reason: General contractors and subcontractors (masons, electricians, plumbers, roofers) are not always the most sagacious and reliable of human beings. Home-building is an unstable business, and the contractor you choose may have only recently entered the field after not having been able to make it as a used-car salesman.

HOW TO BUY OR SELL YOUR HOME

The key to a custom-designed house is the architect. If you make a good choice, almost all your worries are over.

WHAT THE ARCHITECT DOES

A top-drawer architect will show you a sketch of a possible house, provide you with detailed specifications, and supervise the construction so that everything goes according to plan. With such a paragon, you will not need a house inspector to check over the finished construction. Even your need for legal advice will be greatly reduced.

The architect will start off by making sure that your lot has proper drainage and that your house is ideally suited for the lay of the land. He will figure out the best orientation for the house, so that—for example—the living room has a gorgeous view and rooms that need to be especially warm and bright get a southern exposure. He will help you choose contractors, and impress upon you the importance of never paying them more than is warranted by the work they have done. He will insist that you get a "waivers of lien claims" from the builder, so that the subcontractors will never sue you because the builder forgot to pay them. He will remind you to get a "performance bond" from the builder, in case he skips town before the house is completed. The architect may even suggest that you give the builder a bonus if he finishes the house early—and pay a penalty if he finishes late. It's not unheard of.

An architect can also educate you about costs, letting you know, for example, that adding an extra bathroom is pricey, but an extra bedroom is relatively cheap, while one-story houses usually cost more than two-story houses.

Besides which, the architect can get furniture for you at whopping discounts.

For all this valuable assistance, the architect may charge you 10 percent or so of the cost of the house.

Many architects, it is true, have pet ideas, and will try to foist them upon you. But hear them out. They may be right. One architect I know abominates aluminum siding, arguing that it dents easily, doesn't let moisture escape from a house, can give you a bad shock unless grounded, in 10 years' time may need a costly paint job, and prevents firemen from fighting fires. William J. Ward, an architect who has worked for all the leading housing magazines and who has the great good sense to live in Glen Rock, N.J., detests basements, and cannot understand why any sane family would choose to live in a dark and damp hole in the ground. And considering that one out of every four basements leaks, he has an excellent point.

You could, of course, just buy ready-made plans for a house, designed by an architect and circulated in various books and magazines. (No less than Frank Lloyd Wright had his designs for model homes published in *Ladies' Home Journal.*) These plans cost about $150 for a set of five. And since they have been used by homeowners around the country, you can expect few screw-ups. But since you're so close to having a custom-built house, you might as well go all the way.

FINDING A PARAGON

Latching on to a top-notch architect won't be easy. Building private residences isn't especially remunerative for most architects, and not many have much experience. Yet an architect with experience is a must. Just as a surgeon who has performed only a couple of heart bypasses is less desirable than a surgeon who has done hundreds, you want an architect who knows his way around private houses. Some authorities think that 10 years of experience is the minimum you should seek.

For names of architects in your vicinity, write to the American Institute of Architects, 1735 New York Avenue, N.W., Washington, D.C. 20006. Membership is a distinct plus.

Once you have the names of at least three architects, sit down with them, question them about their experience, ask about homes they have designed, the names of the owners and their phone numbers, exactly what work they will do for you, and what their fees will be. You want as detailed specifications as possible—brand, size, color, shape, weight, quality, quantity. You also want the architect to visit the construction site at least once a week, or have a "clerk of the works" do it for him.

Find out what percentage of the architect's designs have actually been built, how many were almost finished on time, and how close the final cost was to the allotted budget.

Check out the houses the architect has designed, and speak to the owners. You might suspect that this is a biased sample—the architect will give you only the names of overjoyed customers—but some people are so nice that they would rather eat ground glass than complain and hurt someone's feelings. So the architect's choices may nonetheless gripe and bellyache to you.

Ask these people some of the same questions you asked the architect. Did bids come close to the estimate? Was the work finished close to schedule? Did the architect help in choosing contractors? Did he closely supervise the construction? What problems have they had living in the house?

YOUR LOT IN LIFE
Unless your builder has lots for sale, you will have to find one on your own. See what real-estate agents have for sale. Drive around town, and outside of town, looking for vacant land.

The neighborhood you choose should be such that the house you contemplate will fit in, with respect to both cost and architecture. If you build a low-cost house in a posh neighborhood, or a contemporary in a sea of Colonials, your new neighbors may pull in their welcome mats.

These days the average cost of a lot is $13,500. But be prepared to pay much more for land in a choice location. A lot that already has utility lines is, obviously, more desirable. If the lot doesn't, see whether your builder will pay for the installation. If you already have an architect, have him inspect the land. He might point out, for example, that if a lot has little or no vegetation growing on it, the soil may be backfill, and the house you build on it may settle severely.

CHOOSING CONTRACTORS
Builders will either have subcontractors on their staffs, or will hire them as needed. Although the former may seem better, according to Ward it doesn't make any difference.

But you do need a builder who is really a builder, not someone who is mainly a carpenter or an electrician, and only builds occasionally. He should have built plenty of houses, and you should, of course, speak with the owners. Check out the builder with the Federal Housing Administration, which has a list of builders who have caused trouble. And touch base with the local Better Business Bureau and your state consumer agency. If the builder is a member of the National Home Improvement Council or the National Association of Home Builders, it's a good sign.

Call the builder's bank and ask about his financial standing. Dr. Sidney Goldstone of Gary, Ind., an authority on housebuilding, says, "I've known people who paid their general contractor $75,000 in cash in advance to build a $100,000 home,

EVERYONE'S DREAM: THE CUSTOM-BUILT HOUSE

and wound up with $50,000 to $75,000 in liens on the house from subcontractors he hadn't paid off."

Beware of the builder who cannot easily be reached by phone. He may be hiding from creditors or complainers. Give points to a builder who lives in the area and whose name is in the name of his company. That builder may take pride in whatever he has built.

Don't make the mistake of having the builder provide you with a house design. The design may be years behind the times, may not recognize the latest in people's tastes or the latest in construction improvements, and may not be suitable for you and your family. The builder should provide insurance against any injuries sustained by subcontractors, and he should guarantee that his work will be "broom clean" when the house is finished.

Any good builder will probably give you some sort of warranty. The National Association of Home Builders has devised a 10-year warranty plan, the Home Owners Warranty (HOW), with these guarantees:

- First year—protects against defective materials and faulty workmanship.
- First two years—protects plumbing, heating, cooling, and electrical systems and their installation, but not against items protected by the manufacturers' warranty.
- First 10 years—protects against any major defects in construction.

For the first two years of the contract, the builder is responsible for the warranty, then an insurance company takes over. The warranty program has no deductible, and coverage is transferable to a new owner. The cost of the coverage is about $3.25 per $1,000 of the selling price, and it's usually included in the price.

For the names of nearby builders offering HOW plans, write to the Home Owners Warranty Corporation, 2000 L Street, N.W., Washington, D.C. 20036.

If a builder you are interviewing doesn't offer the HOW plan, he should provide at least a year's protection on the plumbing, heating, cooling, and electrical systems, as well as on the foundation.

Finally, don't pay any attention to the condition of a builder's fingernails.

You might save some money—5 to 15 percent of the house price—by being your own builder, but I recommend against it. It requires a lot of free time, and often during the day. You have to know a good deal about construction—for example, enough to scream bloody murder if the workmen throw scrap wood under the porch. (You'll get termites.) You have to be a genius at scheduling, so that one workman arrives just as another finishes up. It's risky. And you might not even save money, since a builder can get discounts you can't.

As for the subcontractors, give preference to big companies. They may be more reliable in meeting schedules, their workmen may by some miracle just possibly know what they are doing, and they are more likely to be financially stable. Beware of small firms that give low bids. They may be planning to skimp on quality. Under no circumstances hire anyone on an hourly basis.

Your architect or lawyer can guide you in paying the contractor. Remember, the Golden Rule is to not pay anyone for more work than he has done. Even when the house is entirely finished, you should hold back at least 15 percent until you are sure that all the kinks have been ironed out. A typical payment schedule: 10 percent when the foundation is done; 25 percent for the rough enclosure; 25 percent for the drywall, heating, electricity, and plumbing; 25 percent for the whole job; and 15 percent 30 days after you've moved in.

A FEW CAVEATS
- Get everything in writing.
- Try not to change your mind about anything major once construction is under way. Some builders actually look forward to your asking for extras, because it adds to their profit. "Extras are to builders," says lawyer Stephen Seldin, "what the Colt .45 was to Jesse James."
- The more you know about house construction, the better.
- Keep track of sales taxes on materials your contractors buy. They're deductible from your income tax if you itemize.

Since we started off this chapter with horror stories, it's only right that we end it on a cheery note.

When Harvey Rinzler, a general practitioner from Toms River, N.J., was planning to build a house, he found just the right architect. This is what happened:

EVERYONE'S DREAM: THE CUSTOM-BUILT HOUSE

"On his first visit to our three-quarter-acre home site, this architect sniffed around our naturally landscaped hill like a hound dog on a scent. Then we talked—about those who would live in the house and those who would sleep there on occasion, about the habits and tastes of the immediate family, about the limited area on which the foundation would have to stand, and about how much money we could spend.

"About a week later, our architect returned with sketches for five structures, all of them interesting, none exactly right for us. We listed the good and bad points of each. On his next visit he brought sketches of two buildings we considered more suitable. We chose one, with minor changes. From this point onward, the creative process moved smoothly and easily ahead, absorbing all of us.

"The architect handled the entire process of putting the plans out to bid, and not without difficulties. We found that builders generally avoid unusual contemporary houses. A reasonable bid was accepted after amendment, however, and our architect supervised the construction of the building from start to finish. Any question or complaints we had were directed to him, and through him to the builder. His knowledge of materials and his desire to help us choose the most fitting fabrics, electrical fixtures, harmonizing papers, woods, tile, cabinet styles, and so on resulted in a unique home.

"He found a carved door in Los Angeles, stone for the fireplace in Miami, rough-sawn cedar in Seattle for the siding, a chandelier from Spain, an outdoor lamp from Sweden, slate from Vermont. We could never have done this alone. We disagreed on occasion, sometimes yielding to his professional wisdom, sometimes asserting our own taste.

"We moved into our new home exactly one year after first meeting its designer. The house satisfies all our needs and hopes. It also came within 4 percent of our estimated budget."

CHAPTER

14 *THE SEARCH FOR A REAL CREAMPUFF*

Years ago, I had to buy a house in the vicinity of my ailing parents-in-law, and I narrowed my search to Montclair and Passaic, in New Jersey. After looking at houses in both communities, I came to an inescapable conclusion: You got a better house in Passaic for the same price as a house in Montclair. A newer house, a bigger house, a larger lot, more bedrooms. So I bought a place in Passaic Park, the ritzier section of Passaic. Boy, was it a mistake. I had overlooked the importance of location.

In Montclair I would have had more compatible neighbors, superior schools, better municipal services, more rigorously enforced zoning laws, classier stores. And, not to be forgotten, a house that would appreciate faster.

So the moral is: Given a choice between a Grade B house in a superior location and a Grade A house in an average location, you will usually be better off choosing the former. All this is by way of saying that the three most important considerations in buying a house are—well, you know the answer. Location, location, and location.

Every area seems to have an especially desirable community, a place where the schools are superior, a place where the doctors, bankers, accountants, and writers live—a community with prestige. That's where you should choose a house, or at least in a nearby community that bathes in some of the glow from the prestige community.

If you are moving to an unfamiliar area, the way to identify the prestige community and neighborhood is to ask around. Call a minister, priest, or rabbi in the area. Explain that you are moving and that you need guidance. Ask about schools, local services, local controversies, the best neighborhoods. And ask for the names of informed citizens whom you can phone. If you are taking a new job in the area, pick the brains of your new colleagues. And when you start house-hunting, grill the real-estate agents you meet.

A desirable community will have a top-rank school system. Even if you don't have school-age children, the people you may want to sell to someday, first and foremost, will probably be interested in the schools. Call or visit the school; find out the average class size (the smaller the better); find out whether school budgets have been defeated in recent referendums; ask what percentage of the students go on to college, what the teacher-pupil ratio is, how much per pupil is allotted in the budget, and compare the figures with those of neighboring towns. See whether the school has an enrollment large enough to support programs that are not particularly popular, like Latin, or programs requiring special equipment, such as computer science.

Don't be deceived by high taxes. They can be a good sign. They may indicate that refuse is collected from backyards and doesn't frump up the sidewalks every week. The firemen may be professionals, not volunteers. Snow may be removed promptly, and so may autumn leaves. Of course, a low tax rate doesn't necessarily mean that the town fathers are cheap; it may mean that there's income-producing industry in town. Given two comparable towns, the one with the lower tax rate may be more attractive if industry is responsible—and if the industry is far removed from residential areas.

Once you have zeroed in on a community and a neighborhood, make sure that you can walk to a nearby market if your car conks out. Are playgrounds close? A hospital? A movie theater? Houses of worship? Is there adequate public transportation? How long is it by car or public transportation to the place where you work? An hour should be the outside limit, and time it yourself at the hours when you will drive or commute—don't take someone's word for it. And find out how much it will cost to commute.

EXHIBIT 14-1

NEIGHBORHOOD INSPECTION CHECKLIST

Neighborhood quality   Yes   No
1. Are the homes well taken care of? ☐ ☐
2. Are there good public services (police, fire)? ☐ ☐
3. Are there paved roads? ☐ ☐
4. Are there sidewalks? ☐ ☐
5. Is there adequate street lighting? ☐ ☐
6. Is there a city sewer system? ☐ ☐
7. Is there a safe public water supply? ☐ ☐
8. Are the public schools good? ☐ ☐

Neighborhood convenience
1. Will you be near your work? ☐ ☐
2. Are there schools nearby? ☐ ☐
3. Are there shopping centers nearby? ☐ ☐
4. Is there public transportation available? ☐ ☐
5. Will you be near child-care services? ☐ ☐
6. Are hospitals, clinics, or doctors close by? ☐ ☐
7. Is there a park or playground nearby? ☐ ☐

Neighbors
1. Will you be near friends or relatives? ☐ ☐
2. Will you be near other children of your kids' ages? ☐ ☐
3. Will you feel comfortable with the neighbors? ☐ ☐
4. Is there an active community group? ☐ ☐

Does the neighborhood have any problems, such as:
1. Increasing real-estate taxes? ☐ ☐
2. Decreasing prices of homes? ☐ ☐
3. Lots of families moving away? ☐ ☐
4. Heavy traffic or noise? ☐ ☐
5. Litter or pollution? ☐ ☐
6. Factories or heavy industry? ☐ ☐
7. Businesses closing down? ☐ ☐
8. Vacant houses or buildings? ☐ ☐
9. Increasing crime or vandalism? ☐ ☐

What is your overall rating of the neighborhood?   Good ☐   Fair ☐   Poor ☐

Courtesy: U.S. Department of Housing and Urban Development.

THE BEST TIME TO BUY

The best time to buy a house, supposedly, is in the dead of winter, when owners may be desperate for customers. Actually, it's usually best to go house-hunting when the most houses are for sale—in spring and early summer. You may not save money, but you're less likely to miss out on the house of your dreams. If you can barely afford any house in a prestige community, though, you might shop during the off-season.

DEALING WITH AGENTS

Now that you know where and when to look, it's time to read newspaper ads and start meeting brokers and salesmen.

Here's some final advice about working with agents:

Try to deal with people who have wrinkles and gray hair. Experience is essential. Young salesmen may be bright and charming and all that, but they don't learn the nitty-gritty before becoming licensed. In the 45 hours or so of classes they must take before being licensed, they learn about assessment liens, why listings have to be in writing, and that value equals net income divided by rate of return. They aren't taught the difference between Colonials and ranches, how to obtain mortgage money when it's scarce, and how to deal with a stubborn seller. Older agents may also be less of a mind to get rich quick by showing you three houses and acting as if you're insane because you haven't chosen one of them.

Stress to any agents that you are eager to see houses that have just come on the market, provided that they are in your price range, and no matter what style they are. Houses newly on the market may well be underpriced creampuffs.

GETTING QUALIFIED

Agents will want to qualify you—make sure that you can actually afford the house you say you can. There are few hard-and-fast rules on the subject these days. People are willing to spend more of their incomes on housing, and they must if they want to be homeowners. As vague rules, these will have to do: The house you buy should cost three or maybe four times your annual income. If you are trading up, of course, you can afford more. Don't forget to tally in closing costs—usually 5 to 12 percent of the price of the house—and move-in costs. And your monthly housing costs—principal, interest, insurance, taxes—should not exceed one-third of your net monthly income.

NEW VERSUS OLD

Your agent may also ask whether you want a new house or an existing one. (Agents may favor existing houses; they get lower commissions on new houses.) Tell him you want to see both.

New houses cost about 15 percent more than existing ones because of the rising price of labor and materials. They are usually not located in the best parts of town, and will entail extra expenses for carpeting, curtains, and so forth. But you will get new, modern appliances; better electrical and plumbing systems; and better insulation. You're more likely to be offered a warranty on the house. There will be fewer overall repairs necessary—you may have all of 20 years to enjoy your new roof, for example. The house will probably have what most buyers want these days, from foyers to fireplaces.

There are 50 times as many existing houses as new houses, so they give you more variety to choose from. Old houses were usually constructed with greater care and costlier materials than new houses—the woodwork, especially, may be ornate. Such houses are likely to be better located. They will have mature trees and shrubbery. Because they have been lived in, their faults will be more readily apparent.

THE STYLE OF THE HOUSE

The salesman can streamline his job by having you specify whether you want a Colonial, a Cape Cod, a split-level, or whatnot. You shouldn't have a closed mind on the subject. If I were house-hunting right now, the only house style I would probably avoid is a Cape Cod.

Colonial. This usually means a two-story house. *Advantages:* First-floor rooms and second-story bedrooms are separated, so the kids can snooze while wild parties go on downstairs. You get more space for the money. A Colonial is also less costly to build because the foundation, the exterior walls, and the roof are relatively circumscribed. *Disadvantages:* Second-floor rooms don't have easy access to the outside world—and they are dangerous places to be in case of fire. People are forever climbing up and down the stairs. The stairway itself wastes space. *Overall:* Good for a young family.

Ranch. A one-story house. *Advantages:* Little or no stair-climbing. Adapted to both indoor and outdoor living. The outside is a snap to maintain—from fixing the roof to painting the walls.

The inside is easier to clean, too. *Disadvantages:* Requires a large lot, foundation, roof, and walls. Therefore, costly to build and maintain, costly to heat and cool. And it's hard to have wild parties with the kids sleeping nearby. *Overall:* Good for an older family. But not the style of the future.

Cape Cod. One and a half stories. *Advantages:* Heating costs are low. *Disadvantages:* If the attic is turned into bedrooms, without the attic's insulation the whole house may be too hot in summer and too cold in winter. Second-floor rooms are usually small, ditto the windows. There may not be enough ventilation on the second floor, and there may not be provision for a bathroom there. *Overall:* Not the best idea.

Split-level. The living area is on entry level, and there's a short flight of steps down to the social area, a short flight up to the sleeping area. *Advantages:* A good design for a sloping lot. And because of the design, the flow of interior traffic is smooth. *Disadvantages:* A lot of stair-climbing. Because heat rises, the bedrooms on the top floor may be too warm. Such a house doesn't look attractive on a level lot.

Split-entry. The entrance is just a foyer—meaning that the upstairs and downstairs are normally larger than in a split-level. *Advantages:* The basement is higher than in a split-level, so it has more light. The living area isn't cluttered with traffic. *Disadvantages:* There's even more stair-climbing than in a split-level. The lower level, which is partly underground, may be hard to keep at an even temperature.

Tudor (properly, Elizabethan). Two or two and a half stories, and the stone or stucco walls have half timbers in them. *Advantages:* Has the benefits of a Colonial, along with a striking appearance. *Disadvantages:* According to Henry S. Harrison, a Realtor and appraiser, the eccentric roof angles mean a greater chance of leaks developing. Inside, the nooks and crannies are a housekeeping headache, and are hard to heat and cool evenly. Because of the roof's valleys and peaks, the second-story rooms may be dark and poorly ventilated.

An excellent book on the subject is Harrison's *Houses: The Illustrated Guide to Construction, Design and Styles,* Revised Edition, published by the National Association of Realtors in Chicago.

CLOSER AND CLOSER
Once you have targeted a few houses you're interested in, start comparing them. Take a notebook with you, with a chart like the one in Exhibit 14-2, so all the houses don't merge into one big blur in your mind.

Some other suggestions on house-hunting:

• While corner lots are said to be desirable because the house gets more light, I would be skeptical. Your backyard may have little privacy. You will have a lot of extra snow and leaves to remove from the side sidewalk. And the neighborhood dogs may use the side sidewalk as a dump.
• Be wary of a house on a steep hill. The road may get treacherous in wet weather. Unless you live at the top of the hill, you may have water problems in your basement. And the area may be impossible for bicycling.
• Naturally, avoid a busy thoroughfare. But also be dubious of a street parallel to a busy thoroughfare—drivers may use it as a way of bypassing the busier street. A dead-end street is ideal, even though a lot of drivers will make U-turns there.
• Check out the area within a half-mile radius of any house you're interested in. Be on the lookout for noisy or smelly factories.

GRILLING THE SELLERS
There are a number of basic questions you should ask the sellers, and they are real doozies. If the seller or the agent fibs, you have grounds for a lawsuit later.

First, find out how long the house has been on the market, and whether it was listed before with another broker. If it hasn't moved in a long time, something is probably wrong. A friend of mine bought a house in New York State and soon discovered why it was such a bargain—the neighborhood teenage toughs hung out next to the house.

Find out, if you can, why the sellers are selling.

Find out whether the sellers are getting divorced. Divorces almost always spell trouble in the sale of a house. Spouse #1 may accept your first bid, Spouse #2 may ridicule it. And you have to get both their permissions about which items stay, which are negotiable, and so forth.

Here are more questions to ask, some suggested by Alfred Galfand, a real-estate professor at Rutgers University:

- Is the roof leaking, or has it ever leaked? If it did leak, what damage did it do?
- Is the basement perfectly dry? If it has ever flooded, what damage did it do?
- Do fuses blow or circuit-breakers open frequently?
- Has the heating system ever failed to keep the house warm?
- Has air-conditioning ever failed to keep the house cool?
- What are the heating/cooling costs? (Ask to see the bills.)

EXHIBIT 14-2

COMPARING HOUSES

	1	2	3
Address			
Asking price			
Real-estate taxes			
Water bill			
Heating bill			
Electric bill			
Age of house			
One-story			
Two-story			
Split-level			
Wood frame			
Brick			
Aluminum siding			
Exterior condition			
Storm windows			
Garage/capacity			
Gas heat			
Electric heat			
Hot-water heat			
Age of plant			
Central air/age			
Bedrooms			
Size of living room			

Courtesy: Chicago Title Insurance Company.

- Has the house ever been termite-proofed? What damage had the termites caused? (Most people are overly afraid of termites, which take a long time to do damage. If a house is termite-proofed, it may be protected for 20 years.)
- Are there any easements on the property? Are there any defects on the sellers' title to the property?
- Does the house need more insulation?
- Will there be assessments soon for sewers or repaving?
- Will the house be reassessed for higher taxes soon?

	1	2	3
Dining room			
Kitchen			
Number of bathrooms			
Closets/size			
Refrigerator/age			
Stove/age			
Disposal/dishwasher			
Clothes washer/dryer			
Laundry space			
Water heater			
Basement storage area			
Finished basement			
Attic storage area			
Finished attic			
Number of fireplaces			
Drapes			
Carpeting			
Modern electrical wiring			
Sump pump/drainage			
Public sewer system			
Backyard patio			
Fence on lot lines			
Pleasing landscaping			

HIRING A HOUSE INSPECTOR

Absolutely essential in buying a house, no matter what the price, is getting a house inspector, preferably an engineer, to look it over. He will tell you whether the place is inhabited by termites, whether the heating system is about to give up the ghost, whether there's evidence that the basement has doubled as a swimming pool. You wouldn't buy a secondhand car without having a mechanic look it over, would you? A house costs a lot more than a used car. And don't trust your uncle the plumber or your aunt the electrician. You need someone who knows everything about houses.

I have used a house inspector on four occasions. Once, my engineer pointed out to me that the basement of a house that interested me leaked regularly. That, plus the fact that the house looked smaller every time I saw it, persuaded me to withdraw my offer.

Another time, I put down a binder on a fairly new ranch house—a lovely property next to a gurgling brook. The brook, my engineer informed me, was accustomed to gurgling in the house's basement, too. (I should have guessed from the fact that the basement walls had just been whitewashed.) The roof was also giving out, and it's damnably expensive to replace the mammoth roof on a ranch house. And the two gorgeous bathrooms on the first floor were so close together that the floor underneath was buckling. (A marble placed in the middle of the bathrooms made a line for the sides.) I sorrowfully withdrew my offer.

The house was quickly sold anyway. At the first rainstorm, my agent later told me, the roof leaked a flood and all the carpeting on the first floor was ruined.

For the names of local house inspectors, call or write to the American Society of Home Inspectors, Suite 520, 1629 K Street, Washington, D.C. 20006 (202-842-3096). Expect to pay at least a hundred dollars for an inspection.

A HOME WARRANTY

Even if you use a house inspector, be on the safe side and consider a home warranty.

The majority of people who buy warranties for existing homes are the sellers, not the buyers. It helps them sell the houses for more money, and more quickly. But if your seller has not obtained a warranty for you, get your own.

Check with the National Association of Realtors, 430 North Michigan Avenue, Chicago, Ill. 60611 for the names of approved warranty companies in your area.

There are two kinds of programs:

1. With an inspection. The company guarantees a house's structural soundness and working systems. Charge: $225 to $300 a year.

2. Without an inspection. Only the operating systems are covered. The cost may be $250 a year. Coverage of structural defects may be available at a surcharge.

The period of protection is usually 12 months from the date of the closing. Warranties for new homes are discussed in Chapter 13.

CONTRACT TIME
Don't sign a binder, or preliminary contract, without letting your lawyer read it over first. If you're ornery and don't want to bother with a lawyer yet, make sure that (1) the binder specifies that the earnest money must be returned to you if the inspector finds any significant defects in the house, and (2) the binder itself is subject to the approval of your lawyer.

If your lawyer knows what he's about, these are some of the provisions he will put into the final contract:

- Seller agrees to have the property inspected by a bona fide termite expert prior to settlement, and to provide a report at the time of settlement certifying that the premises are free of termites. If evidence of termites is found, the infestation will be treated and the damage repaired at the seller's expense.
- Seller represents that the roof and basement are free of leaks, and have been so for the past two years. Seller guarantees that all appliances, plumbing, electrical, heating, and air-conditioning systems will be in good working order at the time of settlement.
- Buyer is to arrange for an inspection of the premises by a qualified inspector within five days after the signing of this contract, if he has not already done so. If defects are found, seller must agree to repair them at his own expense, or the buyer has the right to be released from the contract and have his deposit refunded.

- The principals to this contract mutually agree that, in the event of the death of either party, all of its provisions shall be binding upon the decedent's heirs, executors, administrators, and assigns.
- This contract is contingent upon a commitment for financing, described earlier, being obtained by the buyer within 45 days, or this contract will become null and void, and the buyer's deposit shall be refunded.
- Seller guarantees that the property is free of encumbrances except as specified in this contract. Buyer reserves the right to terminate this contract and have his deposit refunded if within 15 days he finds that the premises cannot be used for the purposes intended.
- Seller and buyer are required and agree to make full settlement in accordance with the terms hereof by the date specified. If the buyer should fail to settle by the date specified, his deposit may be forfeited at the option of the seller, in which event the buyer shall be relieved of further liability, or the seller may avail himself of any legal or equitable rights that he may have under the contract. If the seller should fail to settle at the time specified, the buyer may avail himself of any legal or equitable rights that he may have under the contract.
- Seller agrees to assume the risk of loss or damage to the property by fire or other casualty until settlement is held and the deed recorded.

CHAPTER

15 PAY A BROKER TO FIND YOU A HOUSE?

C. Daniel Murr, a real-estate broker in Tucson, Ariz., spent back-breaking months trying to find a mobile-home park for one of his customers. Then he got the awful news: His customer had found his own damn park. Murr wasn't entitled to a commission. He was so miffed that, "just to hurt the guy," he sent him a bill. For $500. And the man, amazingly, paid up. As Murr tells it, he immediately joined the ranks of brokers who think it's a swell idea that they get paid by buyers as well as sellers.

The notion that brokers should work for buyers dates back to the 1960s, but only recently has it begun to make inroads, especially in California and Florida. One broker, Dan B. Warkentin, will even send inquirers the names of three "buyer-brokers" (as they're called) in any of 15 states—not New York or California. Cost: $4. His address is 6641 Backlick Road, Springfield, Va. 22150.

Why pay a broker to represent you when you can hire a broker for nothing? Because, legally, brokers in a traditional real-estate transaction must labor in the best interests of the seller. They must, for example, try to get the buyer to pay the highest possible price. Suppose the seller has priced a house at $210,000, but tells the broker that $200,000 will be perfectly acceptable. If a buyer wants to make a bid, the broker is obliged to urge the buyer to bid $210,000. Or suppose the buyer bids $200,000, but confesses to the broker that he would pay $210,000. The broker is obliged to tell the seller to hold out for $210,000.

If the broker were on the other side, however, he could do the buyer a world of good. He could report which parts of town are the best to live in, how the various schools rank, which houses were built by reputable builders. The broker could reveal what drawbacks he knows about a house—say, that it's in an area notorious for its soggy basements. He could bargain hard for the buyer, not just over the selling price but over who pays the various closing costs, what fixtures stay, and so on. And he could help a buyer track down the best mortgage.

The buyer who pays his own broker thus gets someone to look after his interests. The buyer also gets more houses to choose from than with a seller's broker. A buyer-broker can direct the buyer to houses being sold by their owners, without brokers. An owner selling a house would have no qualms about using a broker if the buyer was paying the freight. Says a buyer-broker in Putnam, Conn., Joseph L. Petrowsky, "We've had 100 buyers as clients in five years, and 20 to 30 percent of the sales have been to owners selling their own property." The buyer-broker can also scout out real estate that isn't being offered for sale. Says buyer-broker William R. Broadbent of San Luis Obispo, Calif., "It's amazing how some owners who had not yet publicly expressed any interest in selling suddenly come to life if they think they can save a commission."

Finally, the buyer may even get his money back. Pay attention now; this is complicated.

Typically, buyer-brokers charge a flat fee—like $1,000 or $2,000; or a percentage of the asking price—like 3 percent; or an hourly rate—like $75 an hour.

Now, a seller promises to pay the broker a commission, usually 6 percent of the selling price. The broker, in turn, is prepared to split that commission with another broker who brings in a real live buyer. The *other* broker in this instance, however, has already been paid—by the buyer. The seller may thus be obligated to pay only a 3 percent commission. Which is why most sellers lower their selling prices by 3 percent—in effect, paying the buyer's expenses. (If sellers refuse—Warkentin calls them "hogs at the trough"—he makes sure the buyers get unusually favorable terms.)

THE BEST PROSPECTS

Who should use buyer-brokers? The ideal prospects are novices to the real-estate game, or people new to an area. But anyone too busy to look at many houses or investment properties might consider it. Obviously, you should hire only a broker who is exceptionally capable, someone familiar with an area, who knows house prices, who can negotiate skillfully and hard.

There is at least one flaw in the buyer-broker concept. The broker a buyer hires will already have houses listed for sale by sellers. And the broker should not represent both buyer and seller in the same transaction. What Daniel Murr does in the rare case when a buyer wants a house that Murr has already listed is to dump one of them. But the point is that brokers may not be eager to show buyer-clients those houses the brokers already have a listing on. Or else they may lose clients.

Maybe the solution is to have brokers specialize in representing either buyers *or* sellers.

CHAPTER

16 *THE CONTINUING SCANDAL OF CLOSING COSTS*

A middle-aged professional man reminisces:

"The first time I bought a house, lo these many years ago, I was unprepared for the closing. The lawyer I used was someone I didn't know at all, recommended by a relative who, as it turned out, didn't know him very well either. It seemed to have taken the lawyer forever to get things ready for the closing.

"The closing itself was traumatic. All those bills! And then there came the lawyer's bill—for $500. He had promised that he would handle everything for $200. In shock, I asked him why he was charging me more. 'Oh,' he said with a coy smile, 'I found I couldn't do it for that little.'

"Later, the knowledge that he had screwed me rankled, and I wrote a letter of complaint to the local bar association, with a copy to the lawyer. The bar association, as is its wont, merely wrote back that I should straighten everything out with the lawyer. Then the lawyer, getting worried, sent a letter to the bar association, with a copy to me, saying that he had told me of the $500 fee—and that he had *also* told me that he was getting a kickback from the title insurance he bought for me. He wanted to cover himself in case I ever found out about the kickback!"

Continued on page 152

AMENDMENT TO APPLICATION

Date _____

LENDER'S ESTIMATE OF SETTLEMENT CHARGES

NOTE: You may apply for the loan in your own name or you may wish your spouse (if any) to be a co-applicant. There is no requirement for your spouse (if any) to apply or otherwise become obligated to repay the debt except to the extent that your spouse's income and/or assets are necessary to qualify you for the loan. However, your spouse may be required to execute the security instrument (i.e., Mortgage or Deed of Trust).

1. Title will be vested in what names? _____
2. How will title be held? (Tenancy) _____
3. Note will be signed by? _____

"GOOD FAITH ESTIMATES"

This list gives an estimate of most of the charges you will have to pay at the settlement of your loan. The figures shown, as *estimates*, are subject to change. The figures shown are computed based on sales price and proposed mortgage amount as stated on your loan application. The numbers listed on the left correspond with those on the HUD-1 Uniform Settlement Form you will be required to execute at settlement. For further information about these charges, consult your Special Information Booklet.

Estimated Settlement Charges

801	Loan Origination Fee	$ _____
805	Inspection Fee	_____
806	Mortgage Application Fee	_____
901*	Interest	_____
902	Mortgage Insurance Premium	_____

EXHIBIT 16-1

THE CONTINUING SCANDAL OF CLOSING COSTS

1107 Attorney's Fees
1108 Title Insurance
1201 Recording Fees
1202 City/county tax/stamps
1203 State tax/stamps
1301 Survey

*This interest calculation represents the greatest amount of interest you could be required to pay at settlement. The actual amount will be determined by which day of the month your settlement is conducted. To determine the amount you will have to pay, multiply the number of days remaining in the month in which you settle times the daily interest charge for your loan.

"THIS FORM DOES NOT COVER ALL ITEMS YOU WILL BE REQUIRED TO PAY IN CASH AT SETTLEMENT, FOR EX-AMPLE, DEPOSIT IN ESCROW FOR REAL-ESTATE TAXES AND INSURANCE. YOU MAY WISH TO INQUIRE AS TO THE AMOUNTS OF SUCH OTHER ITEMS. YOU MAY BE REQUIRED TO PAY OTHER ADDITIONAL AMOUNTS AT SETTLEMENT."

In accordance with the Real Estate Settlement Procedures Act of 1974, I/we acknowledge receipt of the Settlement Costs Booklet. I/we also acknowledge receipt of the notice required by the Equal Credit Opportunity Act which is located on the inside back cover of the Settlement Cost Booklet. By signing this form, we acknowledge receipt this date of a duplicate copy of this form including the "Good Faith Estimates" of settlement costs and the Settlement Costs Booklet with the notice required by the Equal Credit Opportunity Act.

_____   _____
Applicant   Co-applicant

HOW TO BUY OR SELL YOUR HOME

EXHIBIT 16-2

U.S. DEPARTMENT OF HOUSING AND URBAN DEVELOPMENT

SETTLEMENT STATEMENT

Form Approved
OMB NO. 63-R-1501

B. TYPE OF LOAN

1. ☐ FHA 2. ☐ FmHA 3. ☐ CONV. UNINS.
4. ☐ VA   5. ☐ CONV. INS.

6. File Number: 7. Loan Number:

8. Mortgage Insurance Case Number:

A.

C. NOTE: This form is furnished to give you a statement of actual settlement costs. Amounts paid to and by the settlement agent are shown. Items marked "(p.o.c.)" were paid outside the closing; they are shown here for informational purposes and are not included in the totals.

D. NAME OF BORROWER:

E. NAME OF SELLER:

F. NAME OF LENDER:

G. PROPERTY LOCATION:

H. SETTLEMENT AGENT:

PLACE OF SETTLEMENT:

I. SETTLEMENT DATE:

J. SUMMARY OF BORROWER'S TRANSACTION		K. SUMMARY OF SELLER'S TRANSACTION	
100. GROSS AMOUNT DUE FROM BORROWER:		**400. GROSS AMOUNT DUE TO SELLER:**	
101. Contract sales price		401. Contract sales price	
102. Personal property		402. Personal property	
103. Settlement charges to borrower (line 1400)		403.	
104.		404.	
105.		405.	
Adjustments for items paid by seller in advance		*Adjustments for items paid by seller in advance*	
106. City/town taxes	to	406. City/town taxes	to
107. County taxes	to	407. County taxes	to
108. Assessments	to	408. Assessments	to

THE CONTINUING SCANDAL OF CLOSING COSTS

109.	409.
110.	410.
111.	411.
112.	412.
120. GROSS AMOUNT DUE FROM BORROWER	420. GROSS AMOUNT DUE TO SELLER
200. AMOUNTS PAID BY OR IN BEHALF OF BORROWER:	500. REDUCTIONS IN AMOUNT DUE TO SELLER:
201. Deposit or earnest money	501. Excess deposit (see instructions)
202. Principal amount of new loan(s)	502. Settlement charges to seller (line 1400)
203. Existing loan(s) taken subject to	503. Existing loan(s) taken subject to
204.	504. Payoff of first mortgage loan
205.	505. Payoff of second mortgage loan
206.	506.
207.	507.
208.	508.
209.	509.
Adjustments for items unpaid by seller	Adjustments for items unpaid by seller
210. City/town taxes to	510. City/town taxes to
211. County taxes to	511. County taxes to
212. Assessments to	512. Assessments to
213.	513.
214.	514.
215.	515.
216.	516.
217.	517.
218.	518.
219.	519.
220. TOTAL PAID BY/FOR BORROWER	520. TOTAL REDUCTION AMOUNT DUE SELLER
300. CASH AT SETTLEMENT FROM/TO BORROWER	600. CASH AT SETTLEMENT TO/FROM SELLER
301. Gross amount due from borrower (line 120)	601. Gross amount due to seller (line 420)
302. Less amounts paid by/for borrower (line 220) ( )	602. Less reductions in amount due seller (line 520) ( )
303. CASH (☐ FROM) (☐ TO) BORROWER	603. CASH (☐ TO) (☐ FROM) SELLER

Previous Edition is Obsolete

HUD-1 (5-76)

FRONT

HOW TO BUY OR SELL YOUR HOME

EXHIBIT 16-2 (Cont'd)

—2—

L. SETTLEMENT CHARGES

700. TOTAL SALES/BROKER'S COMMISSION based on price $ _____ @ _____ % =
Division of Commission (line 700) as follows:

	PAID FROM BORROWER'S FUNDS AT SETTLEMENT	PAID FROM SELLER'S FUNDS AT SETTLEMENT
701. $ _____ to _____		
702. $ _____ to _____		
703. Commission paid at Settlement		
704.		
800. ITEMS PAYABLE IN CONNECTION WITH LOAN		
801. Loan Origination Fee _____ %		
802. Loan Discount _____ %		
803. Appraisal Fee to _____		
804. Credit Report to _____		
805. Lender's Inspection Fee		
806. Mortgage Insurance Application Fee to _____		
807. Assumption Fee		
808.		
809.		
810.		
811.		
900. ITEMS REQUIRED BY LENDER TO BE PAID IN ADVANCE		
901. Interest from _____ to _____ @ $ _____ /day		
902. Mortgage Insurance Premium for _____ months to		
903. Hazard Insurance Premium for _____ years to		
904. _____ years to		
905.		
1000. RESERVES DEPOSITED WITH LENDER		
1001. Hazard insurance _____ months @ $ _____ per month		
1002. Mortgage insurance _____ months @ $ _____ per month		
1003. City property taxes _____ months @ $ _____ per month		
1004. County property taxes _____ months @ $ _____ per month		

THE CONTINUING SCANDAL OF CLOSING COSTS

1005. Annual assessments	months @ $ per month
1006.	months @ $ per month
1007.	months @ $ per month
1008.	months @ $ per month

1100. TITLE CHARGES

1101. Settlement or closing fee	to
1102. Abstract or title search	to
1103. Title examination	to
1104. Title insurance binder	to
1105. Document preparation	to
1106. Notary fees	
1107. Attorney's fees	to
(includes above items numbers;	)
1108. Title insurance	to
(includes above items numbers;	)
1109. Lender's coverage	$
1110. Owner's coverage	$
1111.	
1112.	
1113.	

1200. GOVERNMENT RECORDING AND TRANSFER CHARGES

1201. Recording fees: Deed $; Mortgage $; Releases $	
1202. City/county tax/stamps: Deed $; Mortgage $	
1203. State tax/stamps: Deed $; Mortgage $	
1204.	
1205.	

1300. ADDITIONAL SETTLEMENT CHARGES

1301. Survey	to
1302. Pest inspection	to
1303.	
1304.	
1305.	

1400. TOTAL SETTLEMENT CHARGES (enter on lines 103, Section J and 502, Section K)

HUD-1 (5-76)

BACK

The closing, of course, is when all the final odds and ends of transferring the ownership of a house are transacted. The buyer winds up with a deed from the seller.

How closings are handled varies all over the country.

In the West, the buyer and seller usually share the cost of an escrow agent, who may be a lawyer or an employee of a title-insurance company. When you use an escrow agent, there is no formal closing with all the parties in attendance. Everything is comparatively simple. If you do use an escrow agent, shop for one who charges a reasonable fee.

Whether the buyer or seller pays for the various expenses also varies by state. But usually the buyer pays. At the closing, the name of the game is Sock It To The Buyer.

The Department of Housing and Urban Development tried to take some of the sting out of closing costs a few years ago by means of the Real Estate Settlement Procedures Act (RESPA), which sees to it that after you apply for a mortgage the lender must give you a reasonable estimate of closing charges, and that one business day before the closing you get a full list of closing costs. (See Exhibits 16-1 and 16-2.) It is certainly not enough time to shop around for bids.

RESPA also forbids title-insurance companies to give kickbacks to lawyers and real-estate agents who refer customers to them. So what the ingenious title-insurance companies did was to make the lawyers agents of the companies. Now, instead of receiving kickbacks, the lawyers receive commissions. And the higher the cost of title insurance to you, the greater the commission they get—a horrid situation known as "reverse competition."

Robert C. Bates, executive vice president of the Chicago Title Insurance Company, tells me that lawyers do a lot of work as agents to earn their commissions. But Robert Hunter, former Federal Insurance Administrator and now president of the National Insurance Consumer Organization in Washington, D.C., says, "That is not my understanding." He adds that title-insurance companies also reward people who refer customers with all sorts of services and other goodies, such as free office space and free typing.

THE BIGGEST SCANDAL

Title insurance is one of the major costs of closing for the buyer, and indisputably the most scandalous.

Title insurance can cover the lender, the buyer, or both, against certain defects in the title of the property the buyer is purchasing. Suppose that 10 years ago a man sold you his house without the permission of his ex-wife. The ex-wife might come along now and demand her dower rights—one-half or one-third—in the house you think you own. Title insurance would pay for the cost of your fighting her claim in court, and also reimburse you if you lost part-ownership of your house.

Lenders usually insist that buyers pay not only for title insurance, but for an "abstract of title" or "report of title." This report lists any limitations on the owner's rights to the property, such as easements, mechanic's liens, or unpaid property taxes. But there are certain defects, like forgeries, that a search will not pick up. That is why you also need title insurance.

And yes, in most communities, you do need title insurance. (Exception: areas that have a Torrens system, where ownership of property is registered, like automobiles.) In fact, if the lender insists that you buy title insurance to cover his mortgage, make sure that you buy owner's insurance at the same time. John Goode, vice president and general underwriting counsel of the Lawyers Title Insurance Corporation, says, "A lot of people see the words 'title insurance' at the closing and go away with the vague feeling that they have title insurance." It will be cheaper if you buy an owner's insurance policy at the same time you buy a lender's policy. And if a seller bought his own policy within the past 10 years, you can get a discount (a "reissue rate") if you buy a policy through the same company. If the seller bought a policy in the past two years, he would then be entitled to a partial premium refund.

A NECESSARY EVIL

You need title insurance because you need insurance, in general, to protect you against the cost of unexpected catastrophes. And finding out that someone else really owns your house or has certain rights to it is a hell of a catastrophe.

Here are some cases reported by the Lawyers Title Insurance Corporation:

The case of the adventurous lady forger

Noticing a vacant house, a woman who "needed funds to continue living her adventurous life" discovered that the owners, an Army major and his wife, were off in Germany.

So she went to the local courthouse and looked up all the information she could on the house. Then she forged a deed making herself the owner, signed the names of the absent owners, and sold the house to an unsuspecting couple.

The couple realized their mistake, of course, when the Army major and his wife returned home and demanded to know what the couple were doing in their house. The couple, fortunately, had bought title insurance, which paid them for their loss. The lady forger was never seen again.

The Pennsylvania man who led a double life

A respectable and prosperous Pennsylvania man bought and sold houses all his life. When he died, it turned out that he had been a bigamist—he had another wife from whom he had never been divorced. The first wife had a claim against every single one of the buyers of the properties that the dead man had owned. It took several different title-insurance companies to pay off all the claims.

Ever meet a walking corpse?

In Chicago, a man vanished for 17 years and was pronounced legally dead. His home was sold. Later the man returned and demanded his property back from the buyers.

In Atlanta, a man was thought to have perished in a hotel fire. After his wife died, his property, too, was sold. And years later, he, too, returned to claim his property. Why had he vanished? "Because," he explained, "my wife nagged me."

Here are other cases from the files of the Lawyers Title Insurance Corporation:

- ▶ The man whom Joe Brown bought his property from had introduced a woman as his wife—and the woman had forged the real wife's name to the deed. Brown had to reacquire a half-interest in his property.
- ▶ Ben Jones had to pay a substantial amount to a "forgotten" son of the man from whose estate he had bought his home. The son was born after the man's will was drawn, and no provision had been made for him in the will.
- ▶ Fred Page had to hand over a substantial check because the man from whom he bought had said he was single. After he died, it was discovered that he was secretly married.
- ▶ Tom Rowe learned that his title examiner had missed a substantial sum in old taxes that had to be paid.

- Sam White had to move his garage because part of it lay on his neighbor's property. The surveyor had erred.
- Bob Smith spent part of a small fortune defending his title when a man who thought, with little justification, that he had better title carried his fight to the Supreme Court.
- Frank Davis found himself faced with a heavy street-paving lien that his title examiner had missed.
- Art Green learned that there was an old mortgage outstanding on his home. A clerk had indexed it improperly.
- Jack Frye lost his property because the signature of one of the previous owners was forged on the deed conveying the property to the man from whom Frye bought.
- David Bell lost his small-business property because it was proved that the man he bought it from was mentally incompetent at the time he signed the deed.

THE TROUBLE WITH TITLE INSURANCE

Now that you are convinced that you need title insurance, let's examine the reasons title insurance isn't exactly manna from heaven.

To begin with, a question-and-answer from a brochure issued by the Lawyers Title Insurance Corporation:

Q. "Do many people actually lose their homes because of title defects?"

A. *"Not if they have title insurance! Title-insurance companies realize that it is most important to the homeowner to keep his home. Therefore, when an insured title is found to be defective, the title-insurance company does everything possible to perfect the title. Most often it is necessary to purchase a claimant's rights in the property and transfer them to the insured. This is practically always possible where only a partial interest is outstanding."*

The *answer* to the question, which seems to have been lost in the shuffle, is a resounding No. Adventurous lady forgers, bigamists' wives, and walking corpses are rare. A 1971 study by Senator William Proxmire found that the risk absorbed by title-insurance companies is "practically nonexistent." Today, the Chicago Title Insurance Company's loss-ratio—premiums compared with actual payouts—is a measly 7 percent. Property and casualty companies have a loss-ratio of 50 percent.

According to spokesmen for the title-insurance companies, they have a low loss-ratio because they have to employ a lot of people. The companies make exhaustive studies of what they shouldn't insure against. This is true as far as it goes. But there is another major reason why title insurance is overpriced: the commissions that the companies pay to lawyer-agents—15 to 25 percent of the premiums.

Another reason why title insurance is overpriced is that there's little or no competition between title-insurance companies. Recently I phoned three title-insurance companies in New Jersey and asked for quotations on insuring my house for $100,000. The first company quoted a figure of $365 for just title insurance, not for the abstract of title. The second company quoted a figure in the general neighborhood: $365. And the third, by an amazing coincidence, quoted a figure of $365.

The fact is that in most states the title-insurance companies have obtained permission to charge the same rates. This isn't a violation of the antitrust laws because insurance is not regulated by the federal government. It's regulated by loopy state insurance commissions.

You can save on the cost of the abstract of title if you shop around, but not much—maybe $50. It will probably be cheaper if you have an abstractor do the search rather than a lawyer.

But on the cost of title insurance, you're probably stuck. Be prepared to pay 0.4 percent of the value of your home. On a $200,000 house, expect to pay $800. Fortunately, it's a one-time charge. Still, if the companies didn't pay big, fat commissions to lawyers, and if there were competition between title-insurance companies, you would pay much less.

It's bad enough that title insurance is overpriced. It's also less worthwhile than it might be. There's a lot that the typical policy doesn't cover, such as defects in boundaries, encroachments, unrecorded easements, unrecorded mechanic's liens, zoning and governmental regulations, rights of parties in possession, and water and mining claims. (A document is *recorded* when it is open for inspection in a town's record office.)

Consumer's Union's *Guide to Public Services* suggests that you ask to have some of these exceptions removed if you buy title insurance, specifically unrecorded mechanic's liens and the rights of parties in possession of your property.

Not only do typical title-insurance policies have standard exceptions; they also won't cover anything resembling an existing imperfection in title. Ron Landsman, a lawyer in Washington, D.C., who is an authority on title insurance, recommends that you fight against any exceptions. "Tell the company that you don't accept those defects they have uncovered," he says. "Try to get them removed."

One long-term solution to the shenanigans of the title-insurance companies is for state insurance commissions to make them compete against one another. Once they start competing, the clever companies will bypass the lawyers, publicize their cheap policies, and really clean up. Another solution, suggested by a government official, is to encourage big, efficient companies like Shearson/American Express, Sears, and Merrill Lynch to enter the title-insurance business.

In the meantime, the best way to handle title insurance is to play the game, but play it well.

The key is your lawyer. Since he is getting a lordly commission out of the title insurance you pay for, he should be willing to charge reasonably for handling the whole closing. Ron Landsman says, "You want someone who will do the settlement for you and whose overall price will be lower. The commission on the title insurance will be incentive enough for him not to charge you a whole lot for the other services." So when you look around for your own lawyer, bargain with him over his price, knowing that he will probably be getting a commission from the title-insurance company.

What if you didn't buy owner's title insurance when you purchased your house? Buy it now, either from the company that you bought mortgagee's insurance from, or from the company that sold a policy to the previous owner. Be sure to get a discount.

If your property has appreciated a lot since you bought title insurance or if you have improved your home, consider an endorsement to increase the coverage. This isn't an automatic step, though. First: Policies issued in recent years by the larger title-insurance companies contain inflation escalators, raising the coverage by 10 percent every year for five years. Maybe you're already covered for the appreciation. Second: Maybe you don't need the extra coverage. The longer you have held the property, the smaller the risk. Robert Bates of Chicago Title reports that there's a nine-year "tail" on title-insurance claims, meaning that after nine years 95 percent of all claims that will ever be made *have* been made. One reason is that claimants die. Third: The cost of remedying most title defects—like boundary disputes—does not amount to the total value of your property.

The last word comes from Chief Justice Warren Burger: "... the basic system of real-estate titles and transfers and the related matters concerning financing and purchase of homes cries out for re-examination and simplification."

OTHER ANNOYING CLOSING COSTS
There are a few other places where you might save money.

The seller may face a prepayment penalty for paying off his mortgage early. He may be able to escape this if he gets the buyer to assume his mortgage (having the lender free him of further responsibility at the same time). Or he may be spared any penalty if he induces the buyer to obtain a mortgage from the same lender.

The buyer may have to pay a loan-origination fee to the lender for the mortgage. According to Consumer's Union, this is unfair if the buyer also has to pay for miscellaneous fees, such as loan applications, credit applications, and notary service. The fee should cover these items. CU also argues that if you pay a loan-origination fee, your mortgage should *not* contain a penalty if you pay it off within a few years. Why should you be penalized if you've paid the cost of preparing the mortgage? As for the cost of the lender's appraisal, CU asserts that if you haven't seen it, you shouldn't have to pay for it: "We believe that if you won't receive a copy of the appraisal report, it's unreasonable for the lender to charge you for it."

The lender may also require a survey. If the seller had a survey made when he bought the house, and it wasn't that long ago, maybe the lender will skip it. If the owner's survey is more than five years old, see whether the lender will accept an affidavit of "no change." If the lender insists on a new survey, ask whether a "visual inspection" will do. That's much less expensive than a full-scale survey. As a last resort, if you must pay for a new survey, have it done by the same surveyor who did it for the seller. The surveyor should give you a discount.

Finally, try not to let the pain of the closing spoil the pleasures of owning a home. Lawyer Stephen Seldin tells the story of a buyer who was suffering through the closing, paying bill after bill in growing dismay. Suddenly, he excused himself to go to the bathroom. He was never seen again.

CHAPTER

17 *THE PERILS OF BUYING A MANSION*

If you're like many other homeowners, you bought the house you're living in for a song, and now you might be able to sell it for a grand opera. You may therefore have been wondering: Since your rather modest home has appreciated like crazy, wouldn't a mansion appreciate like crazy, too? Why not move into a $300,000 home? A $500,000 home?

The answer is that buying a very expensive home is risky, and buying a mansion is extremely risky. The biggest danger is that, because of the thinness of the market for expensive residences even in good times, when you decide to sell you may find yourself house-bound. One man in Wilton, Conn., built a mansion, then offered it for sale for $850,000. Some time elapsed, and he reduced the price to $650,000. After two years and minus a bit of acreage, he was offering it for $590,000. That's like reducing a $70,000 house to $50,000.

The thin market for mansions should be the chief deterrent to anyone's buying a really expensive house—generally defined as one costing $250,000 and up. An ordinary house in ordinary times usually takes four to six months to sell. It typically takes at least a year to unload a mansion.

Another obstacle to buying a luxury house will be finding money. Most lenders have limits on the mortgages they will write for expensive houses. Whatever the amount you want to borrow, you certainly aren't likely to get 80 percent of the appraised value of your house.

Your maintenance costs may horrify you. Jack Merzen of Long Island, N.Y., a house inspector who works for Nationwide Real Estate Inspectors Service, reports that repairmen charge 25 to 30 percent more to fix anything in an expensive house. And W. Fred Mangan, a management consultant in Battle Creek, Mich., reports that a client "who refused to believe that an expensive house would have hidden costs now tells me he dreams of the day he can drive up to it without thinking of the things he and his family had to do without to carry it."

A costly residence may also represent an overconcentration of your assets. Henry S. Miller Jr., an appraiser and real-estate counselor in Dallas, suggests that people with a yen for real estate consider investing in a commercial building instead.

On the other hand, luxury houses have been appreciating nicely in recent years. And the market for mansions has also been spreading out a bit. More and more foreigners have been investing in American real estate, partly because much of it is cheap compared with property in Europe. Another reason given by a foreign investor: "Your country is lagging behind mine by 20 years on the road to socialism. I am buying time."

There's another class of people who will probably always be looking for mansions to buy. One real-estate specialist reports that prosperous gangsters make up a sizable portion of the mansion market. They're easily recognizable by their firm insistence that sellers take cash.

PICKING THE RIGHT AREA

Location is important when you buy any house, but especially important with an expensive one. A $200,000 home in Beverly Hills or Greenwich, Conn., isn't likely to be anything special. Even so, it will probably sell far faster than a splendid $200,000 manor house almost anywhere in North Carolina. Wealthy people tend to want wealthy neighbors.

The wealthy also want diversions, which is why a house near the water, in a hunting area, or in a quality resort area is especially salable. The well-to-do might want to buy it just as a vacation home, or a place to visit when they get bored with their other houses. (The late Joan Whitney Payson, who once owned the New York Mets, also owned seven homes.)

Among foreign buyers, reports Charles Seilheimer, president of the Sotheby Parke Bernet International Realty Corporation, the hunting country of Virginia has the greatest appeal. Not far behind are the environs of Palm Beach and other fancy Florida watering spots, along with the stock-breeding plains of Texas and Georgia.

If you're looking for a house near a city, zero in on name communities. As Irving Price of Hudson Michael Realty in Hudson, N.Y., says, "There'll always be a snob market." Neil King, a real-estate counselor in Skokie, Ill., observes that almost every metropolitan-suburban area contains two or three communities that have prestige, and that "a prestige community is your best safeguard." Lots of land will also guard your investment. Land usually appreciates faster than a house.

PICKING THE RIGHT HOUSE

If the market for mansions is somewhat thin, the market for residential oddities is all but invisible. Most people want to live in center field, not left field. "The average person has pretty conservative tastes," says Alan L. Emlen, vice president of Illustrated Properties. Tom Pretnar of Previews tells of driving through the foothills of Boulder, Colo., a few years ago and admiring the houses he saw—ranches and chalets. "In the middle of them," he says with awe, "was this white, free-form ... *thing*. It looked like it had dropped from the moon. Actually, it was an impressive structure, but in the wrong place. I just can't see the owner ever reselling it unless he meets up with someone just like himself."

Wealthy people are especially prone to self-indulgence where their houses are concerned. The owner and designer of the Connecticut house mentioned earlier, which dropped from $850,000 to $590,000, is a successful architect. His house still hasn't moved—figuratively speaking. What makes it so different is that, literally, it can. The whole house can rotate, from one complete revolution every 48 minutes to one every five hours. By pressing the right buttons, you can admire the sunrise and the sunset from the same room, or keep the same side of the house in sun or shade all day long. A brochure describing the "circambulant" house, as the architect calls it, concludes with the statement that it's "stunning even when standing still." Standing still is what it's likely to be doing for some time to come.

Another example of self-indulgence is furnished by the wealthy owner of a fine old Colonial house in Massachusetts. "He's an antique-car buff," says Joseph B. Doherty of Andover, a past president of the National Association of Realtors. "So he built a $10,000 barnlike structure for five or six of his cars. Then his company transferred him. Not only won't he get his $10,000 back, but he's even having trouble selling the old house. The unsightly barn clashes with it. And people don't like to think about the cost of having it torn down. A photography buff or a stereo nut could do the same thing: Elaborate darkrooms or fancy speaker systems could also scare away customers."

The weirdest house I have ever seen is in Santa Barbara, Calif. Looking at it, you might think that you're gazing through a distorting lens. The brightly colored walls are irregularly curved. What makes the house even more unusual is that (1) it's selling for $1,350,000, and (2) it has only two bedrooms. But the two bedrooms are explainable. Munchkins must live there.

People in the real-estate business have a wonderful term for the truly unique house, the one whose owner has succumbed to the temptation to satisfy all his or her whims and flights of fancy. They call it a "one-owner house."

Besides avoiding self-indulgence, you can also raise your chances of selling your luxury house by buying a newer home rather than an older one. Seilheimer reports that nowadays people are looking for modern conveniences and efficiency—not for the fancy wainscoting and plentiful servants' quarters found in older houses. Even so, he thinks that older houses are often better buys. "In most instances," he says, "you couldn't duplicate an older house for four times the selling price."

ENSURING A SHIPSHAPE HOUSE

It's axiomatic that you should never buy any house until you have it checked out by a professional. Yet an estimated half of all buyers don't do it. Nick Peckovich of Alhambra, Calif., an engineer with Nationwide Real Estate Inspectors Service, says the typical male house buyer—even in Beverly Hills—just knocks on the walls, while the typical female buyer spends her time imagining how her furniture would fit in.

Just because a house has a marble fireplace and 10 bedrooms doesn't mean the roof won't leak or that there are no termites. Some house inspectors report that many homes on the market for $250,000 and more deserve to be condemned.

THE PERILS OF BUYING A MANSION

One house inspected by AMC Home Inspection & Warranty Service in Bound Brook, N.J., was selling for $330,000. What the house inspector found wrong would fill up the remainder of this book. Grumbling, the owner agreed to pay $16,500 for repairs. AMC then made a painstaking study of the cost of bare-bones repairs, covering everything from the leaky basement to the leaky roof. AMC's estimate: $35,000.

Several years ago a prominent New York City obstetrician came into an inheritance and decided to buy a magnificent house. He found one on Long Island for $350,000. Then he asked a friend of his, Paul Waldorf, to visit the house and bring a home inspector along—Waldorf is president of Nationwide Real Estate Inspectors Service. The house was indeed impressive, but there were two problems: No one had lived there for quite some time, so something could have gone wrong without anyone's knowing. And, more ominous, there was a dimly visible three-inch-high watermark all along the basement walls. The doctor shrugged off Waldorf's warnings about the watermark, his attitude apparently being that when you buy a house for $350,000, you don't worry about a little moisture.

Three weeks after the doctor moved in, he telephoned Waldorf. He was almost incoherent. He had discovered the reason for the watermark: There was a leak in the sewage pipe. Right now, the basement was awash with sewage, and his wife was down there mopping it up.

"My wife's ready to kill me!" the doctor cried. "We've been married for 28 years, and I never heard her use a four-letter word before. But now she keeps screaming up at me, 'I'm up to my ankles in shit! I'm up to my ankles in shit!'

"Paul, what did I need this lousy house for?"

A COOK'S TOUR OF VERY EXPENSIVE HOUSES

What might you find inside and outside an all-frills house these days? Well, maybe a special soft-plastic kitchen sink for fine china ... an elevator to the second floor ... a projection room ... a stereo system connected to all rooms, including the bathrooms ... a bathtub in the bedroom, in front of a fireplace ... an indoor fireplace separated by glass doors from the outdoor pool ... heated sidewalks, to melt the ice and snow ... and, above all, lots of land, lots of rooms, lots of space. As the political scientist Harold J. Laski once said, "Americans are prone to mistaking bigness for grandeur."

HOW TO BUY OR SELL YOUR HOME

Here are highlight descriptions of some mansions, palaces, chalets, hunting lodges, and plantations recently sold or for sale by Previews and Sotheby:

Some fancy properties
- "3,727 contiguous acres . . . 10 miles of barbed wire and panel fences around property"
- "Approximately 415 acres with 3,675 feet of beachfront on the Atlantic Ocean [in the Bahamas]"
- "Seven miles of river frontage"
- "Its own 53-acre lake"
- "Artificial waterfall controlled from house"
- "Tiny cemetery with headstones dating from 1790"
- "Pool has underwater speakers for sound system"
- "Property includes natural groves of live oaks thought to predate the discovery of America"
- "Large trees, including 200-year-old oak, each individually lighted, on rheostat controls"
- "Heliport adjacent to the croquet field"
- "Seven-car garage with two apartments"
- "Chapel: 10 pews, with stained-glass windows"
- "Fallout shelter, fully equipped"
- "8,000-foot miniature railroad, 40-passenger capacity"

Some fancy residences
- "28 rooms, 10 family bedrooms, 10 staff bedrooms, 12 full baths"
- "Fireplace a replica of one in the American wing of the Metropolitan Museum of Art"
- "A regulation indoor bowling alley"
- "Balustrade is 19th-century Lord Middleton design, removed from Villa Theresa in Paris"
- "Color TV in all 10 bedrooms"
- "Mink and antique Tibetan rugs"
- "Three stairways to the first floor"
- "Handmade sterling silver shell-shaped sink"
- "Phones in every bath"
- "Has been used as a background for Revlon ads"
- "Recently Paul Newman and Joanne Woodward used it as a location for a movie"
- "200 can be served at indoor buffet luncheons and suppers"
- "Even the garage has oak doors and imported tile flooring"

- "The 45 sumptuous rooms include seven bedrooms plus servants', 17 bathrooms, and 15 fireplaces of marble and wood"
- "The master suite's walls are lined in natural silk"
- "Over 100 paintings, including a Picasso and a Miro"
- "Sixty-one solid-core doors are individually handcrafted"
- "There is an air-conditioned doghouse"
- "Five greenhouses"
- "A fireman's pole from the kitchen to the children's bedroom above"
- "Soda fountain with sink"
- "Thirty miles of electric wiring"

Some fancy taxes
- $14,687 a year [on a $390,000 New York City townhouse]
- $52,824 a year [on a $7,085,000 New York estate]
- $945 a year [the $1,100,000 house is listed in the National Register of Historic Places, so the owner gets a tax break]

The most memorable statement in any of the advertising literature: This mansion has "a warmth not always associated with a 28-room residence."

CHAPTER

18 CONDOMANIA

"I've had clients tell me that they had just signed a contract for a half-million-dollar condominium in Florida without legal representation," says lawyer Stephen Seldin, in shock. Yet even he feels intimidated by the mounds of abstruse documents that condo buyers receive. It's akin to having to read the collected works of Hegel in the original German. "The average deal doesn't pay me enough to read the inch-thick prospectus," Seldin groans.

One of the most common mistakes people make in buying condos or cooperatives, in fact, is not hiring a knowledgeable lawyer. In a pinch, you can call a bank and ask whom the bank uses in real-estate transactions.

There's even more reason to obtain a lawyer when buying a condo or co-op than when you buy a private house. The whole deal is more complicated. And there's little uniformity in condo/co-op regulations from state to state. (Exception: If the FHA is insuring the condo mortgage, it will oversee the building specifications, the bylaws, and so on.)

The rest of this chapter is in a question-and-answer format, just to vary things a bit.

Q. *What's the difference between a co-op and a condo?*

A. I'm glad you started with an easy question. A *co-op* is closer to being a rented apartment than to being a private house. A *condo* is closer to being a private house.

In a co-op, you are a stockholder in the corporation that owns the dwelling. You have a proprietary lease on your apartment—and most co-ops are high-rise apartments in big cities. You own personal property, not real estate. You share the blanket mortgage on the building.

In a condo, you own outright your apartment-townhouse-garden apartment-duplex or whatever. You have an undivided interest in the common grounds—the elevator, the pool, the tennis courts, the parking area, the hallways.

Even closer to the private house is a *planned unit development* (PUD). In a PUD, you own your own dwelling and the ground underneath, and possibly a small yard. You may therefore be responsible for a little outside maintenance, which is rarely the case in co-ops or condos. The grounds in a PUD are supervised and owned by a nonprofit association. Members belong, but don't own shares.

Q. *Which is better, co-op or condo?*

A. A condo.

In a co-op, if a tenant defaults (it happens), everyone must make up the deficit. The same is true of a mechanic's lien—it can be attached against the entire cooperative. In a condo, people are protected because they have individual mortgages and individual deeds. Even if the whole condo goes bust, they're protected.

It's easier to get a mortgage on a condo. Condo mortgages can also be refinanced, and you can get a second mortgage. While co-op loans (not mortgages—co-ops are personal property, remember) are less arduous to obtain than they once were, the interest rate will probably be higher than on a condo. Besides, the board of directors of the co-op may veto anyone who wants to carry a high loan, considering him a special risk.

The relative ease of getting a mortgage on a condo is one reason why condos have appreciated faster than co-ops. Another reason: In some co-ops, you must sell only to the board of directors, and that limits the appreciation.

Condo owners can sell their units more readily. The homeowners' association may have only a right of first refusal, and even that restriction is fading away. In a co-op, the board of directors has the right to approve of whomever you want to sell to—and Richard M. Nixon and Barbra Streisand have been weighed and found wanting. "Some co-ops have slightly nutty boards of directors," says Seldin. "They're so selective, there's almost no one you can sell to."

With a condo, you have more freedom to do what you will to the inside of your unit. With a co-op, the board may object if you renovate. Should you botch up the job and then go into default, the board may have trouble selling your botched-up apartment.

Co-ops have at least one advantage. You can more readily kick out someone whose behavior is objectionable, or someone who is forever behind on his bills.

PUDs may be best of all. They have all of the advantages of condos, and they give you more privacy.

Q. *Do I get tax deductions for mortgage payments and interest with a condo or co-op?*

A. Yes, if they are your residences. You're also entitled to defer payment of capital gains when you sell, and you are entitled to the $125,000 exemption.

Q. *Will co-op/condo life be right for me?*

A. As a dangerous generalization, co-ops/condos are most suitable for small families—and young families. (The old saying is that they are best for the "newly wed and the nearly dead.") Older people may be accustomed to the freedom of private homes. They may yearn for gardens, pets, children, individuality in the outside of their homes, quiet, privacy.

In short, if you have lived mainly in apartments, a co-op or a condo may be a giant step up. If you have lived in a house— and enjoyed gardening and cleaning up snow and leaves—you may be a mite unhappy.

One doctor sold his condo on Miami Beach's Gold Coast and bought a private home in Key Biscayne, explaining: "At the end of a hard day at the office, I like to unwind among my own flowers in my backyard. At the condo, the board set the landscaping rules, and hired gardeners did the work."

Q. *Are condos a fad? Might I lose a lot of my investment?*

A. Good grief, no. Condos, and not the modest detached house, may be the wave of the future. They're cheaper than private houses because they use less land, and the inside space is smaller. They use less energy. They require no lawn care, and as a typical homeowner I can assure you that lawn care is a vastly overrated human activity. Some years back, condos didn't appreciate nearly so much as private homes, but today they're almost neck and neck.

Co-ops may always be an eccentricity. The theory is that they have burgeoned in New York because (1) it's traditional there (Al Smith as Governor gave special tax breaks to co-ops), and (2) snooty New Yorkers are eager to keep the riffraff from moving next door.

Q. *How do I go about sizing up a co-op or condo?*

A. Look at several of them, even those where there are no vacancies or where you are not interested in buying. This will help make you a connoisseur of building designs. Compare their spaciousness, location, provisions for parking, security arrangements, noise levels, odor, maintenance, recreational amenities, storage space outside the units, laundry facilities, and—of course—prices.

According to one rule, there should be only six to eight condo units per acre (43,560 square feet). In a resort area, expect more crowding.

In buildings with elevators, the higher floors will cost more because they will be quieter and have better views. In three-story walkups, the prices of units on the third floor will be significantly less than units on the first and second.

There should be ample provision for parking—two or three spaces per family.

Once you think you know enough to evaluate a condo or co-op, start your intensive research. Talk to tenants. Either have the manager introduce you to some, or brazenly buttonhole those you find walking around. Talk to them for at least 20 minutes—that's when the truth may start to emerge. What problems have there been? Are there lots of units for sale? Have prices been appreciating nicely? Has there been a rapid turnover on the board of directors or homeowners' association?

Find out whether pets are allowed, whether children can live there and not just visit, whether you can rent your unit and for how short a time (some places forbid renting for less than a month). Are most residents young or old? If young, are they noisy swinging singles? If the place is dominated by older people on fixed incomes, they may let the co-op or condo deteriorate by vetoing fix-up expenditures.

Also learn how membership in the board of directors or homeowners' association is determined—by builder's value, market price, size, or equal shares. This shouldn't change. You might be saddled with a higher share of the maintenance fees.

As for the units themselves, check that the soundproofing is okay. Have someone play a radio next door, and listen to how the sound carries. Also, is there a good view? Is the unit too

EXHIBIT 18-1

COMPARING CONDO OR CO-OP UNITS			
	1	2	3
Address			
Asking price			
Real-estate taxes			
Monthly assessment			
Utility bill			
Square footage			
Storm or thermal windows			
Central or individual air-conditioning/age			
Smoke detectors			
Number of bedrooms			
Number of bathrooms			
Separate dining room			
Kitchen eating area			
Closets—number and size			
Refrigerator/age			
Cooking stove/age			
Disposal/age			
Dishwasher/age			
Balcony and/or patio			
Double entry			
Drapes			
Carpeting			

Courtesy: Chicago Title Insurance Company.

near a noisy elevator or trash disposal? Does it have enough natural light? Do you smell cooking odors because of poor ventilation? And check what kind of warranties you get, both on the unit and the place as a whole.

Q. *What pitfalls should I beware of?*

A. If you're buying in a new development, make sure that your deposit money is held in an escrow fund—the builder doesn't commingle it with his own funds. Check that the development is selling briskly, and that it isn't just the units with good views, or the cheaper ones, that have gone. Ascertain what sort of reputation the developer has. How long has he been in business? What other places has he developed, and what are their reputations? What does the local Better Business Bureau say about the developer? Your state Department of Consumer Affairs?

The "Florida problem" refers to greedy developers who retain ownership of recreational facilities and such—like the pool—and charge condo owners to use them. At one building in Washington, D.C., condo owners pay $3,000 extra a year for parking spaces. This trick has been outlawed in many states, but it still exists.

Similarly, be sure that the condo owners own the land beneath the development—it isn't being leased from the developer. That might account for the cheapness of your unit. You will own less than you had thought.

If the property has a professional manager, was he hired by the developer and is it a "sweetheart contract"—one where the manager has two or three years to neglect the place? A short-term contract is always desirable. See whether the manager can be replaced, under the bylaws, by a 75 percent vote of the membership, and not just by a 100 percent vote under the master deed.

If there is a rollover or balloon mortgage on a co-op, is it coming due soon? Your mortgage payments may soar. Also check to see whether assessments for major repairs, like a new roof, are coming up. Large developments may have had independent engineering studies done. Check. In any case, there should be a reserve fund for emergencies—3 to 5 percent of the gross operating budget. Ideally, there will be a limit on the percentage the assessments can be raised in one year. Also see whether any major lawsuits are outstanding—and that the place has adequate fire and liability insurance.

Q. *How about initially renting for a month, to get the lay of the land?*

A. A terrific idea. You may find out where the skeletons are buried, and learn whether life there is really for you. I lived in a Manhattan co-op for a few years, and you had to live there to believe how loudly the neighbors could scream.

Q. *How about buying a co-op or condo for an investment, and renting it out?*

A. Not so terrific an idea. The best co-ops or condos tend to have the fewest rentals. Renters aren't so careful with and concerned about the property as owners are. If you invest in such a place, your investment may not appreciate very much. A top-notch co-op or condo limits the number of renters.

Q. *What about my buying an office-condo for my business or profession?*

A. Office-condos are more and more common these days, and worth exploring.

You won't have to accept steep rent increases anymore—though you will still have rising maintenance costs at your condo. And while rental payments are totally tax-deductible, so are the operating costs, maintenance, mortgage interest, and real-estate taxes you pay with a condo. Besides, for 15 years you get a tax write-off for the depreciation of your unit.

On the other hand, it's hard to expand a condo. What if you want to hire an associate? What if your business blossoms, and you need more space? The top 10 percent of your business income, after all, is probably the most profitable.

If you're lucky, though, you can just sell your condo at a nice profit and buy a roomier one.

Q. *I'm thinking of selling. Any advice?*

A. Estimate your selling price by the prices similar units have been going for recently. It's easier to find the market value of a condo or a co-op than a private house because there's more uniformity.

If your co-op has a management firm that handles sales, give it an exclusive right to sell for a short time—say, a month. Then contact a variety of brokers. Make sure you don't owe a broker a commission if the board of directors nixes your ready, willing, and able buyer.

Offer to sell your unit partly or entirely furnished. It's a strong selling point, especially if buyers are moving across the country.

Be prepared for an early closing. Buyers usually want to move in fast.

Get together all the information that buyers and their lawyers may be interested in—a floor plan, warranties on the appliances, the original prospectus, the current maintenance costs, information on what financing is available, the prices of similar co-ops or condos that have sold recently. Tell buyers honestly what kind of people live in the place, and who your immediate neighbors are. If they seem like serious buyers, introduce them to some neighbors. Your neighbors might appreciate a preview.

And talking of your neighbors, let them know you're selling. They may have friends or relatives they want to move into the place.

CHAPTER

19 IS A VACATION HOME A SHREWD INVESTMENT?

People seem to have either delightful or dreadful experiences with their second homes. In the former category are those who successfully rent their homes when they are not using them, who make friends in the neighborhood and know good repairmen, whose children love the area, and who eventually retire to their second homes or sell out at a stunning profit.

And then there are those people who have dreadful experiences—like me.

We didn't make the mistake of moving in blind. For a summer, we rented in the area. It was charming. What we didn't know was that most people become bored with their summer homes after three years—and three years later, we were bored beyond belief. So we rented the place, through a broker, and it turned out that the renters were the Flem Snopes family itself. They were accustomed to putting nails in doors and walls, careless about keeping us informed about little problems like floods in the basement, and above all neglectful of paying the rent. When we were finally able to evict them—and I don't even want to think about all the trouble it was—we hastily sold the house at a small profit. *Very* small.

We are not the only people disabused by the seduction of vacation homes. Here's what other second-home owners have to say:

▶ "If you can't rent your vacation home most of the year, it becomes a very expensive luxury."
▶ "It's more fun to look forward to a *new* vacation place."
▶ "You'll get saddled with a bunch of freeloading visitors who've come to help you enjoy your summer place."
▶ "Don't buy or build one unless you have more money than you need for prudent living."
▶ "Stay home—and you won't have to complain about being broke all the time, like people who buy summer homes."
▶ "Unless the property is close enough to use every weekend—and sometimes during the week—vandalism and burglary constitute too expensive a risk."

THE BLOOM OFF THE ROSE
In general, vacation homes have lost a good deal of their former appeal. One reason is that the market has been anything but brisk of late, and vacation homes tend to follow the main-home market. Besides, forecasters don't think that the future of vacation homes is dazzlingly bright (see Chapter 1).

Still another reason is that the tax advantages of vacation-home rentals have been drastically curtailed. "The recent law makes the vacation house much less attractive financially," says R.A. Edgar, an accountant in Long Grove, Ill. The law limits the amount of time you can spend in your own vacation house and still write off all your depreciation and maintenance costs. The new rule: If you live in your home more than 14 days or more than 10 percent of the time it is rented (whichever is greater), your write-offs are reduced. "People who buy vacation homes must take a very careful look financially at what it is going to mean," says Edgar. "Today, a vacation home is more of a personal and emotional venture than a financial one."

Then, too, time-sharing (see Chapter 20) has become a keen competitor of vacation homes. People can buy a time-share for relatively little money, and have little or none of the tribulations of maintaining a year-round residence. As Edgar nicely puts it, "If you're looking for a trouble-free existence, a vacation home is not the place to be."

Still, a vacation home can be fun—and if you find the right place it can be a sound investment. Here's some advice:

• Look for a home in an area that is already built up, or has rules against unbridled new construction—like Aspen,

IS A VACATION HOME A SHREWD INVESTMENT?

Colo. That way, your house won't be lost in the bunch when it comes time to rent or sell.
• Seek out a vacation home nearby, so you can reach it without much trouble. You will, after all, be wise to visit your home periodically just to check on whether any problems have developed—like a burglary or frozen pipes. And consider traffic jams when you calculate how far away a place is. My summer home was 45 minutes away in light traffic, three hours away in heavy traffic.
• Concentrate on a glamorous area—like Aspen, Vail, Fire Island, the Hamptons, Cape Cod. It's one of your safest moves. Says Jeanette Smith, director of communications for the American Land Development Association, a trade group, "As with most real estate, if it is well located it can see some healthy appreciation." Places near water, or throughout the Sun Belt, are high on her list of best places.
• Buy or build early in life, when your children are still pretty young. When they become adolescents, the place may begin to pall on them. "Our cabin was fine for our two daughters from infancy till puberty," says one professional man. "Then they got interested in boys—and there just weren't enough boys or activities in that rustic community."
• Plan on trying to rent it out. Evidence that you've rented, even if just once, will make your place more salable. But don't *count* on renting your home. No one knows how many vacation-home owners successfully rent, but the number is probably comparatively small. Another reason to rent, even for a short time: Any income you get from fewer than 15 days of rental escapes taxes entirely.
• When you rent, be very suspicious of tenants. Really check them out. Get references; check their bank balances. And get as high a deposit as you possibly can. Try to rent to one family for as long a time as possible, so you don't have to deal with a variety of people.
• An isolated house is a drug on the market. Be skeptical of any place that is more than five miles away from a town, and give high marks to a place that has public transportation nearby—buses, trains, an airport.
• Look for a house that has year-round attractions—nearby skiing in the winter, swimming and sailing in the summer. Such a place will be more expensive, but it will appreciate more and rent and sell more easily.

- If you buy in a development, find out whether the developer lives nearby—it's a good sign. Speak to other owners about their experiences. If the developer is a giant corporation, you can probably relax. And look for a house that's a little different—better—than the others, so that it will stand out.
- Waterfront property, as you probably know, is especially desirable, simply because there is a limited amount of it. But keep in mind that you may have dampness problems in your house, and its exterior may have to be repainted often.
- Burglaries are a perennial problem. Don't keep anything of great value, real or sentimental, in your vacation house. And try to make arrangements with your year-round neighbors to keep an eye on your place.
- You won't get much of a mortgage when you buy a second home, and whatever you get will probably entail a high down payment and a short number of years, like 10 to 15. Try to get a loan from a lender near your new home. That way, you can start making friends in the area. For the same reason, get a local lawyer.
- You need friends in your new locale. For one thing, you will be able to get recommendations for good plumbers, electricians, and so forth. Good repairmen tend to be rare in vacation areas, as well as everywhere else. If you can tell a repairman "You've been recommended by Smith and Jones," he will suspect you can bad-mouth him to his other customers.
- As with any house you buy, have it checked by a house inspector.
- Don't buy unimproved land unless you know that it has drinkable water. Have a well drilled before the deal goes through. You should get four gallons a minute or you're in trouble. If you won't have sewage lines, make sure that the property passes a percolation test for a septic tank. Have a survey made to see exactly what you're buying. (Buyer and seller usually split the cost.) Finally, check the cost of utilities that serve you, like electricity.
- If you're buying lake property, make sure that access roads are under public maintenance. You would hate to find out, one snowy winter, that they aren't. See what activities are allowed on the lake. Oil spills from motorboats may make swimming unpleasant.
- Heed the old advice about buying in low season and selling in high season.

CHAPTER

20 THE WHOLE TRUTH ABOUT TIME-SHARING

Eugene Sikorski, a general practitioner from Pontiac, Mich., thinks that his time-share in Sanibel, Fla., has "appreciated considerably" since he bought it five years ago. Comparable units now sell for almost double what he paid. He bought four weeks—the last three in August, the first in September—for $22,000. "I like it so much, I've never exchanged," he says.

Chester Godell, an internist in Arlington, Texas, had been visiting the Smokies in Tennessee for 10 years. "All of a sudden, the prices for staying overnight became outrageous," he says. So he bought three time-sharing weeks—in June, October, and January—in different units in Gatlinburg for $4,600 each. He's completely satisfied: "I have a regular place to go, I can exchange it, I don't have to worry about the prices going up."

The success of time-sharing is confirmed by the fact that today it's a $1.5 billion business, and growing vigorously. As recently as 1975 it was a mere $50 million business.

Independent authorities like R.A. Edgar, an accountant and real-estate expert, are also positive. Says Edgar, "Vacation time-sharing can be a good thing for the right person. It's a good deal." And time-sharers whom I interviewed were, to a person, satisfied.

Several years ago, Charles Allen, a dentist in Logan, Utah, spent $3,000 for two weeks in a Park City, Utah, condominium—one week in June and one in November. He has used the exchange service once—last year—for a week in Florida, and was pleased, though disappointed in not getting a place in Cancun or in the Caribbean. His only complaint: Maintenance costs keep creeping up. Last year the weekly charge was $165, and now it's $195. "When we first started, we were told it would be $65 a week."

A Toronto psychiatrist, Albert S. Leung, paid $6,000 for two time-sharing units (summer and winter) at a condominium in Lagoon City, Ontario, two years ago, and last year exchanged one week for condo space in Orlando, Fla. He's happy with the arrangement, and he's thinking of buying another time-share in Florida "because the place there was quite good." His only gripe: The exchange agency "wasn't quick enough—I had to make two or three phone calls to Florida myself."

"The Trouble With Time-Sharing," a recent article in *Money* magazine, tells how expensive it is to travel year after year to your vacation spot, how boring a single place can prove, and how tough it can be to sell a time-share. An article in *Forbes,* "Endless Vacation or Endless Headache?", warns that maintenance charges may skyrocket as properties age, and notes that time-sharing is the leading source of complaints to the Hawaii Better Business Bureau. "The Hazards of Time-Sharing," an article in *The New York Times,* cautions: "You may think you've bought a week's vacation in Shangri-la. But you might end up in the Poconos."

You might easily conclude that time-sharing is an idea whose time has passed, and that time-sharers themselves are a thoroughly disgusted and disabused lot. But the evidence about time-sharing—buying regular vacation time at a resort, a recreational-vehicle park, a yacht, a nudist colony, whatever—suggests otherwise. Time-sharing seems to be blossoming, time-sharers seem contented, and the whole idea seems to have a sparkling future. The press just seems to have been doing its thing—following up an early rash of overenthusiastic stories about time-sharing with a rash of overly gloomy stories today.

SIGNS OF SATISFACTION

The best evidence that time-sharing is thriving comes from a survey that a market analyst, Richard L. Ragatz, recently did

THE WHOLE TRUTH ABOUT TIME-SHARING

for the American Land Development Association, a nonprofit trade group in Washington, D.C. Ragatz surveyed 9,685 time-sharers at 183 projects around the country. Some 86 percent were satisfied or very satisfied with their purchases; 72 percent would have bought the same units again (15 percent were undecided); and an impressive 61.5 percent said that they intended to buy more time-shares.

The chief benefit of time-sharing is that you get a place to vacation every year, with no hassle about reservations. A second clear benefit is that you can exchange your unit for a place somewhere else, so you don't wind up bored with just one spot—as you might with a $200,000 vacation home.

Other supposed benefits are dubious. Do you lock in tomorrow's vacation at today's prices, as the promoters love to say? Well, if you spent $6,000 for a time-share, perhaps you could have invested that money better elsewhere. Then again, perhaps you wouldn't have. In any case, your maintenance costs—typically $140 for a week—will surely keep rising.

Will your time-sharing unit appreciate, and will it be easy to sell? It's too early to tell, but don't be optimistic.

Alan Schlaifer, a lawyer for the Federal Trade Commission, told me: "Evaluate any investment claims made by the seller. The future value of a time-share depends on many factors. Resale of the time-share may be difficult if you face competition from the firm that sold it to you. Local real-estate brokers may not want to include time-shares in their listings. Closing costs, broker commissions, and arranging financing should also be considered. And even if a building increases in value, a one-week time-share, for example, will give you a return of only 2 percent on a single unit and a building." (It's about 2 percent because there are 52 weeks in a year.)

Says David Clurman, a former assistant attorney general for New York who is now engaged in the time-sharing business, "Anyone who buys time-sharing as an investment at this point is off his rocker."

AVOIDING DISAPPOINTMENT

Yes, there are dangers in buying time-shares. At least one project went bankrupt, leaving its investors up in the air. Some of the units now being time-shared are small and seedy hotels in the midst of nowhere. Time-sharing itself has proved so popular that it has attracted the dregs from all types of real-estate sales. But if you have your wits about you, you should be able to navigate the shoals and wind up with a sound purchase.

One question you must answer at the outset is whether you want to own your unit outright, or simply lease it for a number of years—12 to 40 is typical. Leasing has advantages. The unit itself, naturally, costs less to lease than to buy—typically 18 percent less. You don't owe property taxes or mortgage payments, so your maintenance charges are usually less. You won't feel constrained to join a management association, as you might under an ownership arrangement in a condominium. Finally, the developers will probably be more careful about maintenance because the property will eventually revert to them.

The big, big advantage of ownership is that you will gain if the property appreciates over the years—a possibility that by itself makes ownership more desirable. Says Stephen M. Raphael, a New York lawyer who works in the time-sharing field, "You're *much* better off with ownership."

A second key question: Where should you buy? Consider a location not far away. If you're not crazy about exchanging, you won't have far to travel. (The typical time-sharer owns a place within 150 miles of his principal residence.) Also, buying out of state might lead to high probate costs for your heirs.

EXHIBIT 20-1

THE MOST POPULAR DESTINATIONS

If you're thinking of buying a time-share and exchanging it occasionally (most people exchange once every three years), look for a popular destination. And according to one exchange agency, Interval International, these are the areas that time-sharers are most eager to visit:

Winter

Vail, Colo.	Florida
Hawaii	Southern California
The Caribbean	Mexico

Summer

The Northeast	Washington State
Europe	Mexico
Orlando, Fla.	Hawaii

On the other hand, if you're burning to exchange, be skeptical of a place that has only local appeal, the Poconos being a notable example. Look for a glamorous resort in a glamorous area. And choose the high season, but be sure that you know when it is. As Clurman says, "If you accept a time in April in some ski areas, you may have a very interesting vacation in the sunshine, but chances are excellent you won't do any skiing. And you don't want to visit Florida during September or October because all you'll get is a lot of wind." A good clue that a time period is off-season: The price for a unit is lower than for other times of the year.

By the same token, if you're eager to exchange, make certain that any place you're considering belongs to one of the large exchange agencies, like Resort Condominiums International or Interval International. RCI has more members and more resorts. It's a sign of quality for a resort to be a member of either. Neither agency will accept a project in an area where it has enough members already. RCI isn't accepting any more places in the Poconos, for example.

Hire a lawyer to check your contract, but look for one with experience in the field. Says Clurman, "The trouble is that most lawyers wouldn't understand the documents anyway, because they're complex and it's a new field."

Jeanette Smith of the American Land Development Association warns that if you are leasing, and the owner has not paid off his construction loan, you should ask for a "nondisturbance clause." That means you can continue to live in the unit even if the owner defaults. And be sure that, if you own, you have title insurance.

You *must* check out the management of a place before you buy. Speak with other owners; pay an impromptu visit to the unit to see whether it's being properly maintained. Make sure that the managers of the property don't have a lengthy contract—so that if they are negligent they can be sent packing forthwith. "The quality of the management," says Jeanette Smith, "is the big unanswered question for the future of time-sharing."

THE UNCLOUDED CRYSTAL BALL
Talking of the future, what might happen to time-sharing? Will it faddishly fade away? Or will it start giving vacation homes some competition?

Richard Ragatz thinks the latter. In fact, he suggests that well-to-do people in particular consider time-sharing instead of buying a second home. What they might do, he says, is buy a half-dozen quality time-shares in different locations around the world. A well-to-do person living in San Francisco might buy time-shares in Hawaii, Colorado, the Lake Tahoe area, and perhaps in Europe and Mexico. "I would use two or three a year, and exchange the others," he says. "And I would have more variety and flexibility than if I had bought a $250,000 condominium at Tahoe. It's a more sensible purchase."

Unlike vacation homes, time-shares don't call for much expenditure of energy—the whole rigmarole of draining pipes in winter, trying to rent during the summer, and so forth. And, of course, they cost much less.

Ragatz points out, too, that statistics on vacation homes suggest the future possibilities. There are 350,000 time-sharers now. There are 3,500,000 people with vacation homes. "That's a big gap," he says. "It just shows how great the potential is."

CHAPTER

21 HOW TO TELL WHETHER A HOUSE IS WELL BUILT

You won't have a house inspector reconnoiter every residence you look at—only those you are on the verge of buying. So you are going to have to judge most houses on your own. Just don't expect to find a perfect house. Almost all have defects, no matter how exalted their prices. But if a place has an ungodly number of failings, or just a few egregious ones, rule it out.

THE EXTERIOR
A wide lot is better than a long lot, simply because a wide house is more attractive. A regularly shaped lot is preferable to one that is irregular; it will be easier to sell later. A shade tree to the south or southeast of the house will help make the summer heat less oppressive.

A huge front lawn is a waste of space. True, it helps reduce street noise, but a big, private rear yard is better.

It's essential that the area around a house be properly graded, with a slant of about six inches for the first six feet. Otherwise you may wind up with water in your basement.

A driveway that sinks toward the house may also be a problem. Even if there's a drain next to the garage, it may clog up occasionally and let water pour in. A concrete driveway is better than asphalt; asphalt is better than pebbles, gravel, or dirt.

An attached garage has advantages over a detached garage. It lets you bring shopping bags directly into the house, and come winter the car or cars in your garage will get a little heat from the house. A detached garage will probably be old, and in sorry shape. A two-car garage is far superior to a one-car garage; even one-car families can make use of the extra storage space.

If a house has a crawl space underneath, it should be at least two feet high (preferably 30 inches), and the soil should be covered with a layer of concrete or (next best) a plastic vapor barrier. If your house has a foundation and a basement, the foundation ideally will be poured concrete. Concrete block comes second. The foundation isn't the most lovely part of a house, so it should be concealed by shrubbery.

No wood on the house should touch the ground, lest you get wood rot or termites. A sure sign of termites are the narrow mud tunnels they build to reach the ground. But don't reject a house simply because it has termites. Have a termite inspector check how much damage has been done, and have him give you a yearly guarantee. Henry E. Smith, a house inspector in New Jersey, says, "If you eliminate every house that has termites, I know of fine communities where you would eliminate 90 percent of the houses."

The outside walls of a house are commonly made of masonry, wood, or aluminum. Masonry is the high-priced spread, and will need less care than wood. It's fire-resistant, not fireproof. (Concrete can burn.) But the doors and window frames will need maintenance. The mortar between bricks or stones may also need replacing. Probe with a penknife to see whether it's become soft and porous. Masonry, by the way, isn't so good an insulator as you may think. Architect William Ward says, "Wood is better than any masonry. It's an astonishingly good insulator."

Wood siding needs repainting every few years. Check the paint for peeling and blistering. And sight across the house to check how straight the sides are.

Aluminum siding may need repainting every 10 years or so. If your finger is coated with a chalky residue when you pull it across the siding, the 10 years may be up. Push the siding to see whether it has a solid backing, so it won't dent easily. Since aluminum is a good conductor of electricity, aluminum siding should be grounded.

HOW TO TELL WHETHER A HOUSE IS WELL BUILT

A roof with a wide overhang will protect the walls from rain and snow, and reduce cooling costs during the summer. Slate or clay-tile roofs are best. They may last as long as the house. Next come concrete tiles and metal panels, which may last 50 years. Asbestos-cement shingles trail, at 30 years. Asphalt shingles, which are the most common, should last 20 years.

The farther one shingle overlaps another, the better. Use binoculars to check for warped, curled, blistered, pocked, broken, or missing shingles. Examine the granules, which protect a shingle from the sun. If the granules are almost all gone, the shingle's life is almost over. Check whether there are two layers of shingles, the second replacing a worn-out first layer. When the second layer gives up the ghost, you probably won't be able to add a third layer (unless the roof is steeply pitched), and replacement costs will skyrocket.

Wood shingles also last 20 years or so, and shakes (cut by hand, not by machine) even longer. But because they burn readily, many communities ban them. They should have been treated with fire-retardant chemicals.

If there are patches of tar on the roof, the owner has probably been repairing leaks. It's a warning.

Check the flashings—the strips, usually of metal, covering the valleys and openings in the roof—to make sure they are not loose or pitted.

In general, simple roof lines are desirable. And a roof shouldn't have a severely steep pitch. Roofers may have trouble walking on it, and—unless there are snow barriers—snow may cascade down on people. But a roof that slopes too gently may wear out quickly from sun, rain, and wind. A 30-degree angle is good.

If there's no snow on a house in winter, when nearby buildings do have snow on them, heat may be wastefully escaping from the house's attic.

INSIDE THE HOUSE

Doors should open and close easily. Examine the line between a door and its frame to make sure that it is even.

A *foyer* will conserve heat in winter and coolness in summer, and be handy for guests taking off and putting on wraps. A large closet near the entrance is desirable. I wish I had one in my house.

The *kitchen* should be near the dining room, the family room, and the garage. It should be brightly illuminated and have vast storage space. There should be plenty of counter length, at least 24 inches wide, and enough space for a dining nook. The Holy Triangle—stove, sink, refrigerator—should encompass a limited area. There should be an exhaust fan above the stove, which should have a grease guard over it. Henry Smith, by the way, thinks that the kitchen is the key room in a house. Normally, it costs more to remodel an outdated kitchen than to waterproof a basement or replace a roof.

A *bathroom* should be on the same floor as the kitchen, and there should be one and a half bathrooms for every two bedrooms. (A full bathroom has a shower or tub or both.) A bathroom off the main bedroom is a plus.

Flush all toilets to make sure that they work efficiently. Remove the cover on the back of the toilet and check the flotation arm. If it's bent downward, repairs will have to be made. Make sure the guts aren't corroded.

Visit the highest bathroom in the house, turn on all the faucets, and flush the toilet. If the faucet water slows to a trickle, you may have a problem with water pressure or blocked pipes. Check, too, that the water drains quickly.

The caulking around the tub and inside the shower stall should be in good shape. Otherwise, water may have leaked down, rotting timber under the tub or eroding the pan under the shower.

Interior bathrooms are better, because you won't have cold walls. Such bathrooms should have exhaust fans. Check the rooms below all bathrooms to see whether the ceilings show water damage.

The *fireplace* should have an ashbox, for easy cleaning. If there are no signs that the fireplace has been used recently, the owners may have found that it smoked. Fireproof flooring should extend 18 inches in front of the fireplace, one foot to each side. Make sure there's a damper that operates.

The floor of the *garage* should tilt toward the outside, so that you can easily hose it down. The garage itself should have a window, and one door besides the main door. There should be a convenient electrical outlet.

The *basement* shouldn't smell moldy or musty. Check the walls for cracks. If the cracks have been filled in, you can tell how often—and how bad the settling is—by the discoloration of the material used. Any crack one-third of an inch wide is worrisome. A vertical crack isn't as bad as a horizontal crack. The former may simply indicate uneven settling of the house; the latter may mean that the foundation wall is buckling.

To check for water problems, see whether the nails in the walls' baseboards (if there are any) are rusty, and whether the floor tiles have white stains at the joints. These are merely clues, though. The boiler or water heater may have flooded once or twice. "The only way you can really tell whether a basement leaks," says Smith, "is to be there when it's raining." But a favorable sign that a basement is dry is that good furniture is kept down there.

To check for termites, look not only for mud tunnels but also for discarded insect wings and for wood so soft that you can poke a screwdriver into it.

You shouldn't have to walk through one *bedroom* to get to another—or, for that matter, through *any* room to get to another. (After the Lindbergh baby was kidnapped, many homes were built so that no one could leave the nursery without cutting through another bedroom.) A bedroom should have windows on two different walls, for cross-ventilation. Bedroom closets should have four feet of rod space per family member.

Check the *attic* for signs of discoloration on the ceiling, indicating leaks. There should be adequate ventilation, either through louvers or a window. If the attic is finished, the insulation should be in the ceiling; if unfinished, in the floor. Six inches of insulation are adequate.

WINDOWS, WALLS, FLOORS
"Casement windows," says Sherman Price, a house inspector in New York City, "stink." Casement windows are typically those metal jobs that work with a crank. The trouble with them is that they rust, become warped, and create condensation. Wooden casement windows are another story.

Make sure that all windows open and close easily. If the windows pop out for cleaning, all the better. Storm windows should have "weep" holes on the bottom to let water escape.

To check the floor, jump up and down on it. Too much springiness may be a problem. If the floor has a carpet glued over plywood or concrete, walk heavily on it and listen for a snap, indicating poor adhesiveness. You can usually gauge the quality of any carpet by the density of the pile.

Walls in older homes may be plaster, while those in newer homes are probably drywall (gypsum board). Plaster deadens sound better, but cracks more readily. The best drywall is glued to the wood studs, not nailed to them, because the nails have a tendency to pop. A drywall should be half an inch thick, not just three-eighths of an inch. If the walls are paneled, push against them to make sure they are thick enough. Quarter-inch panels are desirable, not just one-eighth of an inch. Insulation in the walls should be at least three inches. You may be able to check by removing a light-switch's cover and using a flashlight to see the insulation.

ELECTRICITY
These days you need 150 amperes and 110/220 volts coming into a house. If the service panel doesn't show the amperage, you're safe if there are three wires coming into the house from outside, or 10 to 12 wires leaving the service panel.

Circuit breakers are better than fuse boxes. With circuit breakers, you can easily reconnect the electricity after chasing down the cause of the break. And you can't "overfuse" a circuit breaker. If a house has a fuse box, a large package of fuses nearby suggests that fuses blow frequently.

Aluminum electrical wiring installed before the early 1970s may be a fire hazard. Such wires have AL stamped on them. Have an electrician inspect them.

Electrical outlets throughout a house should be 12 feet apart or closer, the reason being that most electrical cords are six feet long. Normally, every room should have four outlets. Ideally, outlets will be at the corners of walls, so they are easily accessible with furniture in place. Three-pronged (grounded) outlets are advisable, to protect against shocks.

The electrical switches in the bathrooms should not be reachable from tubs or showers. It's especially important here that outlets be grounded.

A light-switch should be near the front door, easily accessible as you enter. There should be outside lighting in the back and front to discourage burglars. Both the front and the back of a house should have weatherproof electrical outlets.

HEATING
Whether oil or gas is more expensive depends on your area. But electrical heat is almost always the most expensive. Still, build-

ers like electrical heating because it's easy to install. And it does have advantages—it burns cleanly, and it can be regulated for individual rooms. It may be the fuel of the future.

Heat is usually distributed by water, air, or steam. Water has the advantage that it remains in radiators longer, keeping rooms at an even temperature. The cycles of warm-air heat may make room temperatures fluctuate. Also, with water you have less need for a humidifier. On the other hand, the ducts used with warm air may be adaptable for central air-conditioning. And with warm-air systems, you can filter the air to some degree.

If you have a warm-air system, registers will supply heat and grills will return cool air. The registers should be on the outside walls, the grills on the inside walls; both should be near the floor, so you won't be hit with drafts. The presence of dark stains on the registers may be a sign of a malfunction in the heating system.

There should be at least one heat source for every outside wall in each room.

The heater itself should be as new as possible. If it's the old-fashioned type, covered with asbestos and shaped like a mushroom, you may have to replace it soon.

The thermostat should be located where it's not unusually warm or cold—not next to a register or where it gets blasts from an open outside door.

Even if it's summer, turn up the thermostat to see how quickly the heat comes on. If there are odors from leaking oil or gas, or excessive vibrations, start worrying. Be especially careful that rooms that have been added on to the house get enough heat. Also pay special attention to rooms over a garage and to rooms on the corners of a house.

The water heater should have a minimal capacity of 50 gallons for a family of five, 40 for a family of four, 30 for a family of three. These heaters usually have a life of at least 10 years. Try to learn when a heater was installed; the date may be on the heater itself. Look for rust on the heater's seams. And check how quickly the water in the house gets hot.

PLUMBING

Examine the area around the pipes for wet spots on the ceiling, floors, and walls. Check the pipes themselves for rust, mineral deposits, wetness, and discoloration.

If the pipes are made of different metals—copper here, galvanized iron there—it's a sign that the owner has been replacing them. Further replacements may be needed soon.

The longest-lived pipes are made of copper or brass, not galvanized iron. But the line connecting the house drainage pipes to the main sewer should be iron. You can readily tell whether a pipe is copper or bronze. These metals are not magnetic; iron is. Copper and bronze pipes also have soldered joints, while iron pipes have threaded joints. Older houses tend to have bronze pipes. As for the new plastic pipes, most engineers think highly of them. The best pipe systems in general are the most direct, with the fewest sharp angles.

All sinks, toilets and other fixtures should have turn-off knobs underneath, so that you can make repairs without turning off the water at the main line.

The best faucets tend to have the manufacturer's name on them. The manufacturer is proud of them.

It's a decided minus if a house has a septic-tank system, not a public sewage system. (Although that $8 million house owned by a rock impresario in New Jersey, mentioned earlier, has a septic tank.) In fact, septic-tank systems deserve a whole chapter unto themselves.

CHAPTER

22 HOUSEBREAKING YOUR SEPTIC TANK

Most Americans don't know a septic tank from a hole in the ground. People who buy houses in the outlying suburbs or the country, beyond the reach of community sewage-treatment plants, rarely check to see whether the septic-tank systems are in good shape. Even the 20 to 30 percent of the population now living in houses with individual sewerage systems usually know next to nothing about the care and feeding of septic tanks. In fact, the first response of many homeowners, upon being told that their septic tanks are all fouled up, is "What's a septic tank?"

What the owner of a septic tank needs to know, first of all, is that a hole in the ground is a cesspool. Cesspools are large, covered excavations, often lined with building blocks, into which all the household sewage pours. Unless the soil is very porous, cesspools tend to clog up with solids and bacteria after a few years; if the soil is too porous, sewage may even contaminate groundwater and springs used as sources of drinking water. Understandably, many communities in this country forbid the construction of new cesspools and refuse to permit old ones to be repaired.

A septic tank is a marvelous improvement over a cesspool. It can keep solids and bacteria from quickly clogging up the soil or polluting the water supply. The initial cost of most do-

---

This chapter is reprinted from the June 1974 issue of *Money* magazine by special permission; © 1974, Time Inc.

mestic systems depends on such variables as labor costs, local competition, and the rockiness of the soil. If properly installed and maintained, a system can last 20 years or more without giving trouble; one in a house used only during the summer can last indefinitely.

A septic-tank system is designed to capture most of the solids from house sewage inside a watertight receptacle underground—the tank itself. Bacteria inside the septic tank digest some of the solids, turning them into gases and water and thus reducing their volume. Because these bacteria live without free oxygen, they are called anaerobic. The word "septic" refers to the activities of such bacteria. Partially clean water—called effluent—flows out of the tank into a drainage field. This may be a deep seepage pit similar to a cesspool or, more likely, a trench field made up of long perforated or open-jointed pipes buried in shallow gravel-filled trenches.

On its best behavior, a septic-tank system calls no attention to itself with odors or sluggish plumbing. The ground over the tank and its drainage field totally conceals the unpleasant fact that sewage is being treated on the property. Only the property owner and the municipal health department know—or at least ought to know. But living with a septic tank is not so free and easy as living with a house that sends its sewage into a municipal system. Waste water from the laundry, kitchen, and bathrooms cannot be limitlessly drained away as though into an abyss. Bulky paper and bits of plastic refuse should be kept from going down the drains at all.

In practice, perhaps as many as 50 percent of all septic-tank systems do not work properly, causing both heavy expenditures and personal anguish. The chief sanitary engineer for the Colorado Department of Public Health, William N. Gahr, claims to speak for most members of his profession when he says, "We wish we had never heard, or never would hear, of the septic-tank method of sewage disposal."

Anyone who has his druthers should choose a house connected to a public sewer. Unfortunately, lots of good residential territory is not going to be blessed with sewers for many years, if ever. House-hunters venturing beyond city sewers in search of places to live can save themselves monumental inconvenience, to say nothing of monumental expenses, by learning about the construction and care of septic tanks. When septic-tank systems fail, the trouble is usually that they were installed in unsuitable terrain, or were improperly built, or died from a combination of neglect and repeated insult. To begin your education, get a copy of the sanitary regulations of the health or pollution-control department of the state in which you're looking for property.

THE LAY OF THE LAND
First make sure that the property is suitable for a septic-tank system. The soil should be readily permeable. The groundwater level and bedrock or other impermeable deposits should be at least four feet below the bottom of the trench field or seepage pit. Low areas should be avoided, because after a rain all the water may flow there. Also avoid land that slopes more than 15 degrees: Water will flow too rapidly through the pipes.

The property should be large enough to provide for a second drainage area should the first one clog up. By the time the second one gurgles to a halt, the first can probably be used again. If, as is likely, the homeowner will obtain drinking water from his own well, the water supply should be 75 to 100 feet away from the drainage area. To support a typical septic-tank system, a property with its own well should measure a minimum of 20,000 square feet, about half an acre. Houses connected to a municipal water supply may need only half that.

To make sure that a piece of land fits these requirements, the buyer should have a civil engineer examine the ground and do a percolation test, which consists of pouring water into various holes on the property and observing how quickly the water is absorbed. Unless the soil can absorb at least an inch of water per hour, it may not be suitable for a septic-tank system.

The best place for a septic tank is in the front of the house. With the waste line located there, it will be easier to connect the house to a public sewer if one ever comes down the road, and the septic-tank cleaner's pumper truck will have ready access to the tank. But to avoid contamination, wells should be upgrade from drainage fields. Therefore, if the property is on the downhill side of the street and if it also has a well, the sewerage system may have to be in back and the well in front. If the sewerage system *must* be built in the backyard of a house under construction and a municipal sewer line is just a few years away, have an additional sewer connection built in front. Perhaps you can also save a few hundred dollars by getting approval for a temporary cesspool instead of a septic tank.

THE TANK ITSELF

The best septic tanks are made of concrete. Steel tanks, which usually cost about the same, last only 10 years or so, while concrete tanks may last as long as the houses they serve. The optimal size for a tank is determined by the number of bedrooms in the house. For one or two bedrooms, tank capacity should be 750 gallons; for three bedrooms, 1,000 gallons; four bedrooms, 1,250; five or six bedrooms, 1,500. These figures allow for garbage grinders, automatic dishwashers, and washing machines.

Grease traps—boxes to capture grease before it enters septic tanks—are usually not needed for residential disposal systems. Nor are special seepage pits needed for home laundry equipment. Rainwater, however, should be channeled away from septic tanks and drainage fields.

Most septic-tank systems include a "distribution box" between the tank and the drainage field to equalize the flow of effluent into the pipes of a trench field or into a series of seepage pits. The Government Printing Office's *Manual of Septic Tank Practice* is opposed to the distribution box, no matter how you sluice it. Such boxes, the Public Health Service maintains, tend to tip over and become maldistribution boxes. But many state authorities favor the use of a distribution box, provided it is installed very carefully.

THE DRAINAGE FIELD

With most solids removed, household sewage can be safely drained into a cesspool-like seepage pit or trench field. In choosing between the two, keep in mind that trench fields cost a bit more than seepage pits but also last longer. Being near the surface, trenches permit some of the effluent to evaporate and some to be carried off into the roots of grass and flowers. Loosely packed earth around the pipes also promotes drainage, but heavy equipment cannot be operated over a trench field without risk of crushing the pipes. Seepage pits need much less area. A typical trench field occupies 1,000 to 2,000 square feet, whereas a seepage pit may need only 50 square feet.

The size of any drainage field depends on the soil's percolation rate and the number of bedrooms in the house. The more trench area above the minimum needed, the longer the trench field will last, so be generous. There are limits, however: Some experts say that trenches should be no longer than 60 feet; others say 100 feet.

Sanitary engineers disagree over whether the pipes in a trench field should be sloped. If the ground is fairly level, the best thing to do is probably to have the pipes level, too, and have their ends interconnected. That way, if one end of a pipe becomes blocked, effluent can still enter it through the other.

INSPECTING EXISTING SYSTEMS

My family and I once foolishly rented a country house with septic-tank problems. We always refer to that house as our Waterloo. To avoid the crises we suffered through, anyone thinking of buying a house with a septic-tank system already installed should take certain precautions. Your first task should be to find the tank. Many property owners don't even know where it is. Some people do have a map, or there may be one on record with the local health department. If the homeowner you are thinking of buying from doesn't know where his septic tank is, start being dubious. Septic-tank pumping companies may charge $50 an hour to search for a tank. As sometimes happens, a lovely patio may have been built over the tank—a patio that will have to be ripped up so that the tank can be cleaned. Usually, though, a septic tank is easy enough to find, because typically it is five or 10 feet from the house sewer line. You can find it by poking an iron pole into the ground. The top of the tank should be no more than a foot below the surface.

Try to find the results of any percolation tests done on the property, the capacity of the septic tank, and the type and location of the drainage field. Ask when the septic tank was last pumped out. Tanks should usually be pumped every three to five years, but most people never have their tanks inspected and have them pumped only when there is trouble.

Next, challenge the system. Flush all toilets three times in succession. Run five inches of water into the bathtub and watch it drain away. Pay attention to whether all the water goes down quickly. Then visit the lowest drain in the house—the basement shower, say, or the laundry sink—to see if water has backed up into it as a result of your upstairs tests.

If the system withstands your water torture, it may not matter when the homeowner last had his septic tank pumped. Even if water backs up into the house during your test, you need not immediately cross the home off your list. Perhaps it's simply that the line from the septic tank to the drainage field is blocked. If you're really interested in buying the house, ask the owner to have the trouble checked. You should be there when the workers investigate.

Inspect the grounds around the house for effluent or raw sewage; it's not unusual to find wastes from a defective system oozing out of the soil above the drainage field. Even if you don't see escaping sewage, note whether any section of the lawn is much greener than another. Areas where the grass is thriving too conspicuously may be irrigated by leaking effluent.

Telephone the local health officer to find out whether he has cited the house or others in the neighborhood for emitting raw sewage or odors in violation of the sanitary code. Ask whether he has a record of when the septic tank was last pumped out. Finally, ask neighbors within a five-house radius whether their sewerage systems have been functioning smoothly.

If you do see effluent or sewage escaping above the drainage area, all your worries may be over: You probably should not buy the house. Replacing a drainage field can cost almost as much as building a whole septic-tank system for a new house. In a landscaped yard, septic-tank crews have to work very carefully, often forgoing the use of heavy equipment.

MAINTAINING THE SYSTEM

If you buy a house with a septic-tank system, you will have to learn to conserve water. Don't toss a cigarette into the toilet and flush it—that wastes five gallons. Have leaky faucets fixed immediately. Don't do two or three loads of laundry in one day; space out the washing over the week.

Be especially stingy at times of the year when heavy rains or melting snows saturate the ground, reducing its ability to drain away waste water. At such times, have small children double up in the bathtub; take all your washing to a laundry. In Northern states, winter is another time to be cautious. The water in your drainage field may freeze if nobody uses the plumbing for a week or two. Frozen drainage will cause sewage to back up into the house. Worse yet, many septic-tank companies close up shop during the winter because new houses are rarely built then, so you may have trouble getting emergency repairs. To prevent winter freeze-ups, some people spread hay, plastic sheeting, or snow over the drainage area.

Be sure that nothing that isn't biodegradable enters the septic tank. The plastic in disposable diapers and sand from a cat box will fill a septic tank all too quickly. Also keep bulky paper waste out of the septic tank—sanitary napkins, paper towels, and so forth.

Flushing yeast or store-bought enzymes into your septic tank to aid the bacteria is pouring money down the drain. "Good old Mother Nature takes such good care of you," says Peter J. Smith, chief of the residential sanitation section of the New York State Department of Health, "that you don't need this garbage."

Introducing caustic chemicals into a septic tank to soften the solids is akin to setting fire to a house to thaw out the pipes. The chemicals may soften the solids inside the tank, all right, but the solids may then float out into the drainage field and resolidify, clogging the field. Salt water is another thing that can shorten the life of a drainage field. The salt solution used to recharge water softeners should be piped to a special seepage pit. To protect the bacteria inside a septic tank, be careful about what chemicals you pour down the drain. For example, photographic chemicals should not go inside a septic tank. Don't fret, though, about the moderate use of disinfectants, bleaches, and drain cleaners.

The only chemical ever recommended is copper sulfate (blue vitriol), which kills roots threatening to clog drainage pipes. Don't let shrubbery or other vegetation with long roots grow above a trench field.

The septic tank should be inspected once a year and pumped out if necessary. The trouble is that many septic-tank pumpers will choose to empty a tank even if it could go safely unpumped for another year or more. Pumping is usually more profitable than letting matters rest for a small inspection charge. Inspecting the tank yourself is not one of the joys of homeownership, but you can do it, and save money, by following the advice in any standard guide.

When the tank is being pumped, have as much of the contents as possible removed. If the sludge at the bottom is hard, the pumper should stir it with a stick. Peer into the tank to make sure it is empty or nearly empty. The tank need not retain any solids to keep bacteria flourishing; even in an empty tank there are more bacteria than you would care to count.

To conserve bacteria, though, discourage the pumper from pouring disinfectant into an empty tank. In the North, have a tank pumped in the late spring or summer, so that bacteria will have several warm months to proliferate before cold weather slows their growth. Don't let a pumper run water into a tank to wash it out, either, because he may charge you for pumping that water out again. "The tank does not need to be flushed or hosed down," states John H. Pomeroy, a sanitary engineer with the U.S. Department of Agriculture, "but rather emptied."

If you don't already have a map of your septic-tank system, make one as soon as you find the tank. Record the distance of the tank from two fixed objects—a corner of the house and a tree, for instance. You might also place a marker on the ground above the septic tank—a birdbath, perhaps, or maybe a shrine to Pluto, god of the underworld.

CHAPTER

23 THE RETIREMENT SPOT THAT'S BEST FOR _YOU_

Choosing a place to spend your retirement is like choosing a spouse. In both cases, you should be wary of acting on impulse, and instead weigh the alternatives carefully. You shouldn't be seduced by mere good looks (a sunny climate), but seek out depth as well (varied activities). And you would be wise to get a gander at your intended in the early morning (off-season) as well as during a formal dinner party (high-season).

Picking a retirement place and picking a mate are also subjective choices. There's no accounting for tastes. Just as someone married Phyllis Diller, there are well-to-do individuals who retired to Cleveland, Ohio, and Centerville, Iowa. (We'll meet them later.) Dr. A. Smith Kinne, who retired to Stuart, Fla., points out that "I love the ocean, but this area might not appeal to somebody else. You get a professional city guy, who's lived in big cities all his life, and he comes to a semirural area like Stuart and is bored—and scared. He wants to be back with the noise, the pollution, the traffic. It's _home_ to him."

But while choosing a mate and a retirement place are very much matters of taste and temperament, there are certain suggestions we can make, beginning with:

Don't overestimate the weather. From what one is forever hearing, one could get the impression that the key person to consult before retiring is a meteorologist. And all that stands between you and perfect bliss during your retirement is discovering the spot with the perfect temperature and humidity. All this, truth to be told, seems to be hoopla churned out by Sun Belt chambers of commerce.

Norman D. Ford of Boulder, Colo., author of *Where to Retire on a Small Income,* believes that the weather is overrated: *"Activities* are what you want." In agreement is Leo Baldwin, housing consultant for the American Association of Retired People, who says, "Weather is what we talk about, but many people who move because of benefits they expect to derive from the climate eventually return to the Northern states because of other factors—closeness to friends and relatives and so forth."

As for retirees themselves, Dr. H. Close Hesseltine, 80, who retired to Centerville, claims that "there's no perfect place in the world, where all the seasons are equally good." Granted, "It's a little cold in Centerville during the winter, but it's better than *northern* Iowa."

Dr. Donald R. Hayes, who retired to Georges Mills, N.H., thinks that winters there "are all right if you don't have to get up at 6 in the morning. You keep warm, drive four-wheel-drive vehicles, burn the wood you cut yourself in your wood stove—I tell you, it's great!" As for the lure of the Sun Belt, "I think they're crazy, sitting around in the sun all the time and playing golf. I was going to play golf when I retired, but I find I don't have the time."

A younger man, 59-year-old Dr. Andrew D. Kerr Jr. of New York City, says, "As long as I'm healthy, I don't mind the cold weather at all. I've managed to get along lo these many years. I do very much enjoy the change of seasons, such as the cold snappy weather in the winter." Dr. Kerr plans to retire to upstate New York to run a dairy farm he owns.

Dr. Evelyn L. Parsons, 75, who retired to Wellesley Hills, Mass., says of the cold winters: *"That's* when you thank heavens you're not practicing anymore. I don't enjoy the very cold weather, but I don't have to go out in it."

Dr. Isaac Horowitz of Fairfield, Conn., a humorous man who is still active in medicine at age 69, says, "We have perfect weather here. We have spring, summer, fall, and winter." As for those icy blasts of December, "I push the thermostat up. It's no problem. In America, you make your own weather."

Don't move where your children are. This is a mistake because all too often, once you're living near your children, they move. "We'd like to see more of our children," says Dr. Kinne. "We're down in Florida, and they're in the Chicago area. We manage to go up there three or four times a year, but maybe it's a good idea to be separated from them, to help them develop their own personalities and their own lives." Dr. John Post of Elko, Nev., puts it this way: "We don't want to butt into our kids' lives, and we don't want them to butt into ours."

Norman Ford has a clever solution. Move to a resort area, a tourist attraction. Then the kids will be eager to visit. "You won't have to pursue them, they'll pursue you," he says.

Consider your spouse. All too often, the husband moves wherever he has dreamed of retiring, ignoring his wife's wishes. His wife dutifully accompanies him. Once there, she mopes and gripes. Eventually something gives.

The best way to deal with this problem is to emulate what Dr. Lester D. Bibler did. Dr. Bibler, who says he is crowding 80 now, had practiced in Indianapolis but loved Florida. He had friends there. For 30 years, he paid dues to keep up his license to practice in Florida. Mrs. Bibler, alas, didn't relish Florida's heat and humidity. So they remained in Indianapolis. And he and his wife, who have been married for 60 years, "are still speaking," he reports.

Do research well in advance. According to Peter A. Dickinson, who has written extensively on retirement, there are six yardsticks by which to measure retirement places:

1. Climate and recreation.
2. Cost of living.
3. Housing.
4. Medical facilities.
5. Recreation and culture.
6. Special services for seniors.

Have two or three retirement places in mind, and see how they stack up against these criteria.

Some other steps to take: Rent for six months in a location before buying there, or before selling your original home. Spend your vacations there year after year, to meet the local people—lawyers, bankers, doctors. Subscribe to the local paper, or perhaps to just the weekend edition. Says Leo Baldwin: "You'll learn about unusual weather, the price of real estate, the price of hamburger meat, the kinds of shops, the kinds of entertainment, problems with the transportation system. It's one of the essential parts of research."

Make sure your retirement area attracts your kind of people. A person without an academic background might feel out of place with a flock of retired school teachers, and so might a doctor who moves to an area dominated by retired lawyers. If it's a tennis-playing or boating crowd, you might feel like an outsider if neither sport is a passion of yours.

The right way to go about finding a retirement area was demonstrated by Dr. John Post. He is one of the few retirees I have spoken with who retired to an area far from his roots. He went from Chicago to a small Nevada town.

Over a period of years before he retired, Dr. Post and his wife visited Ohio, Arizona, New Mexico, Texas, Mississippi, Florida, Nevada, Michigan, California, and Oregon. They were already familiar with Florida and Hawaii. They wound up in Elko, Nev. "It was just what we wanted," he says. "We haven't regretted it for a minute. It's just beautiful country, and from our house we have a complete view of the mountains. The weather is wonderful, and we're able to go outdoors practically every day of the year. And there's a lot to do around here—rock-hunting, ghost-town searching, golf, fishing, hunting—it's all here. We didn't know a soul when we moved out here eight years ago, but the people are extremely friendly and, good gracious, it's been just fabulous for us."

In short, don't choose a retirement place at the last minute. The time to start looking, evaluating, and comparing is years before you retire. If you marry in haste, you may repent at leisure.

Consider two places. If you can swing it, keeping two houses is a smart deal. That way, you can be close to your old friends and acquaintances part of the year, and still have the novelty and excitement of a new destination. You also have more choices of the weather you want. And, if you're lucky, you can rent out

THE RETIREMENT SPOT THAT'S BEST FOR YOU

your retirement home while you're back at home base. "It's the ideal thing," says Peter Dickinson. "More and more older people, in fact, are buying second homes as investments and renting them out six months of the year."

Many prosperous people keep two homes during their retirement. Dr. William Loeb lives in Cleveland, but come winter he and his wife travel in their recreational vehicle to Florida. "I enjoy being in Cleveland in the winter," he says, "but I feel more comfortable when it's 75 degrees and I don't have to put on a coat and boots to go places."

Choose a diverse place. Even if you love golfing every weekend, you may get tired of golfing every single day. Don't make the mistake of thinking that any one interest of yours will occupy you throughout your retirement. That's one reason there should be diverse activities wherever you go.

There's another reason. Most people go through two different retirement stages. The first is young-old age, when they remain active in sports and other outdoor activities. But then they pass into old-old age, when they become fragile. The energetic life of the typical retirement spot—Sun City—then becomes somewhat unsuitable.

In response to the need, enclaves for the old-old are springing up outside Sun City itself. Says Leo Baldwin: "There are a number of housing developments outside Sun City, with access to the city, where a person can buy a home in a quiet, residential area, cultivating friendships within Sun City and participating in Sun City activities as much as he chooses. But without the former personal investment in Sun City." In other words, a diverse place.

Still another goal is age variety. Says Norman Ford, "It gets pretty gloomy if you're isolated among old people who are constantly getting sick and dying off. You need the stimulation of young people." As someone has said, you should always live in an area where you can yell at a kid who takes a shortcut across your lawn.

Consider sitting still. Most of the retirees I recently interviewed chose or plan to choose retirement spots close to their roots. In this, they reflect the general population. Leo Baldwin points out that 70 percent of people over 65 will die occupying the same residence they lived in when they reached 65. Of the 30 percent who move, 23 percent will not go more than 25 miles away from where they lived earlier. Only 3 percent will move out of the state in which they reached 65 or took up retirement.

It is the lure of family, friends, and familiarity that keeps retirees, even prosperous ones, in place. And Baldwin defends their decision: "Very few people appreciate how difficult it is for an older person to change doctors, attorneys, butchers, dressmakers, banks, and churches. They become accustomed

EXHIBIT 23-1

THE BEST—AND WORST—STATES TO RETIRE TO

The three worst states to retire to, according to a study by Chase Econometrics, are Massachusetts, Maine, and New Jersey. The three best: Utah, Louisiana, and South Carolina.

Chase Econometrics, a subsidiary of the Chase Manhattan Bank, ranked 48 states as retirement havens, skipping Hawaii and Alaska for lack of data. Points were assigned according to a state's economic conditions, taxes and living costs, weather and utility rates, demographic trends, and housing and services.

This is how the states ranked and the number of points they earned:

Ranking	State	Points
1	Utah	305
2	Louisiana	295
3	South Carolina	280
4	Nevada	260
5	Texas	230
6	New Mexico	200
7	Alabama	185
8	Arizona	175
9	Florida	160
10	Georgia	155
11	Colorado	140
12	North Carolina	110
13	Tennessee	100
14	Kentucky	88
15	Virginia	75
16	Washington	40

THE RETIREMENT SPOT THAT'S BEST FOR YOU

to people they deal with on a day-to-day basis, and if they move, they become nostalgic for these old connections."

Retirees who plan to remain where they are eloquently defend their choices. "My own philosophy," says Dr. Donald Hayes of Georges Mills, "is that when you have a wide circle of friends, to suddenly pick up and go to Florida, California, or what have you, to make new friends all over again, doesn't seem very smart." Says Carl Wiesel, 67, a psychiatrist in Lex-

Ranking	State	Points
17	California	35
18	Oklahoma	30
19	Maryland	− 5
20	Idaho	− 15
21	Oregon	− 15
22	Kansas	− 20
23	Arkansas	− 63
24	Mississippi	− 70
25	West Virginia	−103
26	Wyoming	−130
27	Nebraska	−138
28	Ohio	−160
29	Wisconsin	−170
30	Delaware	−195
31	Indiana	−195
32	Illinois	−223
33	Missouri	−225
34	Pennsylvania	−230
35	South Dakota	−235
36	Iowa	−240
37	Michigan	−245
38	Montana	−250
39	Minnesota	−265
40	North Dakota	−280
41	Connecticut	−285
42	New Hampshire	−300
43	New York	−355
44	Rhode Island	−373
45	Vermont	−385
46	New Jersey	−390
47	Maine	−428
48	Massachusetts	−498

ington, Ky., "I don't know too many people who just pack up and take off to start a new life. I think it's much more sensible to stay where you know people and enjoy living."

Says Dr. Horowitz of Fairfield: "It's the natural thing to do. I don't think you make new friends late in life. They're just people you see on the street. You don't have that warmth. For instance, I've been out of high school for 50 or 60 years, and I have a very peculiar, very personal relationship with my high-school classmates still. I don't have that sort of relationship with anyone I've met in the past 20 years."

Besides, there are few places in America that don't have their own charm.

Says Dr. Loeb of Cleveland: "My family has lived here for over 130 years. It's home base. And Cleveland is the only city I know of with this number of single-family-occupied housing units. As opposed to New York or Chicago, where everything is nose to tail, there's space here. And remember, when you say 'Cleveland,' you're thinking of the inner city, but it's part of a five-county area. Besides, I've been in the Southwest, and I feel more comfortable with the big deciduous trees and greenery here. And I'm busy all the time. Teaching at Case Western Reserve, attending conferences, working around the house, doing some photography, a little fishing."

The doctor who retired to Centerville, H. Close Hesseltine, moved there from Chicago to be with his sister, his closest living relative. "It's a nice place, and I was raised in the county west of here," he says. "It's a stable community; people here have a respect for community responsibilities."

Dr. Wiesel, who hasn't retired yet, praises life in Lexington: "You have all the cultural advantages of living in a college town. There's something going on all the time. And while you can enjoy small-town life, we're only 80 miles from Cincinnati and Louisville if you're looking for excitement."

"It's God's country," says Dr. Horowitz about Fairfield. "I'm an hour from New York; there's a summer theater 25 minutes away. I'm on Long Island Sound, and I have a motorboat. I have skiing, sunbathing, everything. The Sun Belt? I don't know what I'm going to find there that I don't have here. California is a strange country, I'm not at home there. I see only old faces in Florida. I want to believe that I'm still young."

If a person retires where he has been working, it's not difficult for him to keep employed.

THE RETIREMENT SPOT THAT'S BEST FOR YOU

Dr. Horowitz, who at 69 has not retired, makes a strong case for continuing to work: "Why should I stop? As long as I'm on this earth, I want to be useful. And I'm still a better radiologist than any snooty young guy who comes along. I'm a good radiologist, and if I do my work I'm doing my patients a favor. So I practice for my enjoyment—and for the benefit of the patient. It gives me a certain amount of satisfaction. I'm not just occupying a place on earth and taking someone's bread away for no good reason.

"Most doctors who have retired found practicing a chore, or only did it to make money, or had a limited perspective, so they didn't mind stopping work. They didn't get the ego satisfaction that practitioners like us do. You have an ego trip when somebody sees you on the street and says, 'Doctor, you're wonderful!' You think you are a real somebody," he says with a laugh.

Dr. Wiesel, who plans to practice part-time when he retires, says: "Most of us feel we'd go nuts if we quit entirely—unless we had an avocation of some sort that would be just as fulfilling."

To Dr. Loeb, continuing to work is an insurance policy. "Who the hell knows what's going to happen? The economy might fall apart, my income might disappear, there may be a need for me to have some income."

People who retire to the same place where they've been living are, of course, doing the equivalent of marrying their childhood sweethearts. And it's not a bad idea.

The final suggestion is:

Don't live with a mistake. If the retirement place you choose doesn't prove to be Shangri-la, don't think you are tied to it forever. You can always pack up and leave. It happens again and again. Peter Dickinson tells about a group of people from Rochester, N.Y., who went down to Florida together and spent their time there discussing events and people back home. Eventually they wised up and fled back to Rochester.

In short, keep in mind what Dr. Loeb said when we began chatting about the similarity between choosing a spouse and choosing a retirement place: "The big difference is that it costs a lot less to switch your retirement place."

APPENDIX:

A CONCISE GUIDE TO THE NEW MORTGAGES

This list of new mortgages and the commentary were prepared by the Federal Trade Commission.

TYPE	DESCRIPTION
Fixed-rate mortgage	Fixed interest rate, usually long-term; equal monthly payments of principal and interest until debt is paid in full.
Flexible-rate (floating-rate) mortgage	Interest rate changes are based on a financial index, resulting in possible changes in your monthly payments, loan term, and/or principal. Some plans have rate or payment caps.
Renegotiable-rate mortgage (rollover)	Interest rate and monthly payments are constant for several years; changes possible thereafter. Long-term mortgage.
Balloon mortgage	Monthly payments based on fixed interest rate; usually short-term; payments may cover interest only with principal due in full at term end.
Graduated-payment mortgage	Lower monthly payments rise gradually (usually over 5–10 years), then level off for duration of term. With flexible interest rate, additional payment changes possible if index changes.
Shared-appreciation mortgage	Below-market interest rate and lower monthly payments, in exchange for a share of profits when property is sold or on a specified date. Many variations.
Assumable mortgage	Buyer takes over seller's original, below-market-rate mortgage.
Seller take-back	Seller provides all or part of financing with a first or second mortgage.
Wraparound	Seller keeps original low-rate mortgage. Buyer makes payments to seller who forwards a portion to the lender holding original mortgage. Offers lower effective interest rate on total transaction.
Growing equity mortgage (rapid payoff mortgage)	Fixed interest rate but monthly payments may vary according to agreed-upon schedule or index.
Land contract	Seller retains original mortgage. No transfer of title until loan is fully paid. Equal monthly payments based on below-market interest rate with unpaid principal due at loan end.
Buy-down	Developer (or third party) provides an interest subsidy that lowers monthly payments during the first few years of the loan. Can have fixed or flexible interest rate.
Rent with option	Renter pays "option fee" for right to purchase property at specified time and agreed-upon price. Rent may or may not be applied to sale price.
Reverse annuity mortgage (equity conversion)	Borrower owns mortgage-free property and is in need of income. Lender makes monthly payments to borrower, using property as collateral.
Zero-rate and low-rate mortgage	Appears to be completely or almost interest-free. Large down payment and one-time finance charge, then loan is repaid in fixed monthly payments over short term.

APPENDIX

CONSIDERATIONS

Offers stability and long-term tax advantages. Interest rates may be higher than with other types of financing. New fixed rates are rarely assumable.

Readily available. Starting interest rate is slightly below market, but payments can increase sharply and frequently if index increases. Payment caps prevent wide fluctuations in payments but may cause negative amortization. Rate caps, while rare, limit amount total debt can expand.

Less frequent changes in interest rate offer some stability.

Offers low monthly payments but possibly no equity until loan is fully paid. When due, loan must be paid off or refinanced. Refinancing poses high risk if rates climb.

Easier to qualify for. Buyer's income must be able to keep pace with scheduled payment increases. With a flexible rate, payment increases beyond the graduated payments can result in additional negative amortization.

If home appreciates greatly, total cost of loan jumps. If home fails to appreciate, projected increase in value may still be due, requiring refinancing at possibly higher rates.

Lowers monthly payments. May be prohibited if due-on-sale clause is in original mortgage. Not permitted on most new fixed-rate mortgages.

May offer a below-market interest rate; may have a balloon payment requiring full payment in a few years or refinancing at market rates, which could sharply increase debt.

Lender may call in old mortgage and require higher rate. If buyer defaults, seller must take legal action to collect debt.

Permits rapid payoff of debt because payment increases reduce principal. Buyer's income must be able to keep up with payment increases.

May offer no equity until loan is fully paid. Buyer has few protections if conflict arises during loan.

Offers a break from higher payments during early years. Enables buyer with lower income to qualify. With flexible-rate mortgage, payments may jump substantially at end of subsidy. Developer may increase selling price.

Enables renter to buy time to obtain down payment and decide whether to purchase. Locks in price during inflationary times. Failure to take option means loss of option fee and rental payments.

Can provide homeowners with needed cash. At end of term, borrower must have money available to avoid selling property or refinancing.

Permits quick ownership. May not lower total cost (because of possibly increased sale price). Doesn't offer long-term tax deductions.

GLOSSARY

abstract of title A document itemizing the transactions affecting a property's title, including sales and liens, mortgages, or other encumbrances.

acceleration clause A provision in a mortgage that the lender may, under certain conditions, demand immediate payment of the balance of the debt.

adjustable mortgage loan (AML) A floating-rate mortgage offered by federally chartered savings and loan associations and savings banks.

adjustable-rate mortgage (ARM) A floating-rate mortgage offered by federally chartered commercial banks.

affidavit of title A written declaration of clear title of ownership by the seller of a property, sworn or affirmed to a notary public or similarly authorized official.

agent One who acts for another, as in buying or selling a property. A real-estate agent is either a real-estate broker or a real-estate salesman.

amortization The gradual repayment of a loan, incorporating interest and increasingly reducing the principal.

assessed valuation A judgment for taxation purposes of a property's financial worth.

assessment A charge levied against property to fund such community improvements as streets and sewers.

assumption of mortgage The takeover by a purchaser of the existing mortgage on a property.

balloon-payment mortgage (balloon mortgage) A mortgage in which the principal must be paid off in a lump sum at maturity, even if payments have been based upon a longer-term maturity.

GLOSSARY

basis For tax purposes, a figure arrived at by adding the value of improvements to a property's original cost.

binder A preliminary payment and contract for the purchase of real estate.

blanket mortgage A mortgage funding the purchase of more than one piece of real estate.

blend mortgage A new mortgage whose interest rate is higher than that of the existing mortgage but lower than going mortgage rates. Also, a wraparound mortgage arranged by a lender.

broker Someone who, for a fee or a commission, negotiates sales, as of real estate. A real-estate broker has his own office, unlike a real-estate salesman.

building code A community's regulations governing new construction.

certificate of title A document attesting to the ownership of a property.

chain of title A chronological record of all transfers of ownership of a given piece of property, compiled from public records.

chattel An article of personal property, such as a chandelier, not permanently installed in a house.

clear title A title that is clear of encumbrances, and therefore marketable.

closing The meeting between buyer and seller at which title is transferred.

closing costs The expenses, such as lawyers' fees, incurred in transferring a title to a property, but not including the property's actual cost.

closing statement A written account of all the expenses pertaining to a real-estate transaction.

cloud on title Any claim on a property's title, such as a lien, that tends to diminish the owner's ability to sell it.

condominium (condo) A dwelling in which each unit is owned by an individual rather than by an overall landlord,

GLOSSARY

and in which the unit-owner has an interest in the common areas. Also, a unit in such a dwelling.

conventional mortgage A mortgage not insured or guaranteed by a government agency such as the FHA or the VA.

conveyance The transfer of property title. Also, the document, such as a deed, by which title is transferred.

co-operative (co-op) An apartment house owned by its residents, usually as shareholders in a nonprofit corporation, and managed by an elected board of directors. Also, an apartment in such a building.

creative financing Novel ways for a buyer to afford to purchase a property, usually calling for financial assistance from the seller.

deed A written, sealed instrument conveying title to real property.

default Failure to fulfill an obligation, as to make mortgage payments.

deficiency judgment A judgment calling for payment of the balance of a mortgage-secured debt not satisfied by foreclosure and sale.

demise A transfer of lease for a number of years. Also, to make such a transfer.

due-on-sale clause A statement in a mortgage contract specifying that if the property is sold, the balance must be repaid immediately, and a new buyer cannot assume the mortgage.

earnest money A deposit accompanying a signed offer to purchase a property.

easement A right granted to an individual or a company to use property, as, for example, to install utility lines.

encroachment An extension of a building or other installation beyond its owner's property line onto another owner's property.

encumbrance A restriction on a property, such as a claim, lien, or zoning regulation, that limits its value or use.

GLOSSARY

equity The value of a property in excess of any encumbrance such as a lien or mortgage.

escheat The reversion of property to the state in default of legal heirs or claimants.

escrow Documents, money, and the like, pertinent to a transaction, placed in the custody of a third party until certain conditions are fulfilled. Also, the withheld state of such materials, which are said to be "in escrow."

escrow account A trust account maintained by real-estate brokers and lawyers for the deposit and disbursement of escrow funds.

escrow agent A neutral party who has custody of documents and money placed in escrow.

exclusive agency An arrangement whereby one real-estate broker has the sole right, besides the owner himself, to sell a property for a specified time.

exclusive right to sell A right to sell granted to one real-estate broker, and committing the owner to pay that broker a commission should the property be sold, by anyone at all, during the time of the contract.

Federal National Mortgage Association A privately owned organization subject to regulation by the Department of Housing and Urban Development that buys and sells mortgages and other securities in the secondary mortgage market. Also called Fannie Mae.

fee simple Outright ownership of real estate, the only restrictions being governmental, as in zoning ordinances. Also called fee simple absolute.

FHA-insured mortgage A mortgage with repayment guaranteed by the federal government, through the Federal Housing Administration.

fiduciary A person acting as a trustee. Also, held in trust, as in "fiduciary possession" of property.

first mortgage The first lien, in mortgage form, placed on a property pledged as security.

fix-up costs Costs incurred by a homeowner to spruce up his property 90 days before sale, deductible from the adjusted sale price in computing capital gains. The costs must be paid within 30 days after the sale.

flashing Strips of metal or other protective material used to cover joints or angles, as of walls and roofs, for waterproofing purposes.

floater Insurance that covers movable property, and covers it wherever it goes.

floating-rate mortgage A mortgage whose interest rate varies according to an outside economic index, such as the interest rate on five-year Treasury obligations.

foreclosure The procedure by which a mortgagor in default is deprived of his interest in and right to redeem mortgaged property.

for-sale-by-owner agencies Real-estate agencies that will help a homeowner sell his house himself, for a charge less than the traditional agency's commission.

foundation The supporting construction, wholly or partially below ground, of a building.

graduated-payment mortgage A mortgage allowing for initially low but increasingly higher installment payments of both interest and principal.

grantee The buyer in a real-estate transaction.

grantor The seller in a real-estate transaction.

ground lease A lease conveying the use of the land. Also called land lease.

growing equity mortgage A new mortgage being offered by Merrill Lynch in which the interest rate is fixed, but monthly payments can vary. Any increase in the payments helps reduce the principal owed, not the interest.

gutters Channels along the eaves of a roof that carry away rainwater.

hypothecate To pledge a property as security for a debt without transferring its title; to mortgage.

improvement An alteration that "materially adds to the value" of a house, "appreciably prolongs its useful life, or

GLOSSARY

adapts it to new uses" (IRS definition). The cost can be added to the tax basis of a house in computing the seller's capital gains. See *repair*.

installment contract An arrangement whereby a buyer obtains a loan from a seller, but does not receive title to the property until the loan is mostly repaid.

interest-only mortgage A mortgage providing for payment of interest alone until the date of maturity, upon which the principal must be paid.

junior mortgage A mortgage, such as a second mortgage, that can be paid up only after holders of prior mortgages are paid in full.

land contract A written agreement to transfer real estate upon the fulfillment of certain conditions. Also called agreement of sale.

lease-option An arrangement whereby a prospective buyer lives in the seller's house and pays rent, and has a right to buy the house in the future. In some cases, the rental paid is applied toward the purchase price of the house.

lien A legal claim on a property as payment of or security for a debt or charge.

lis pendens A legal document giving notice that a suit is pending.

listing A written agreement authorizing a broker to rent or sell another's property. Also, the property itself.

listing broker The real-estate broker who first contracts with a homeowner to sell his house.

marketable title A title free of encumbrances and defects.

market value A property's value in the open market.

mechanic's lien A lien against land and buildings favoring workers who have furnished either materials or labor for their improvement.

metes and bounds A description of the footage and boundaries of real property.

MGIC Mortgage Guaranty Insurance Corporation, the largest private mortgage-insurance corporation, and the first of its kind to be opened after the Depression.

mortgage A legal document conveying a loan to be repaid with interest, and secured with a pledge of real property.

mortgage commitment A written notice from a lender agreeing to grant a mortgage on a specified piece of property for specific terms.

mortgagee The holder of a mortgage; for example, a lending institution.

mortgagor The borrower.

multiple listing An arrangement among brokers to share their real-estate listings, and providing for the sales commission to be shared by the listing broker and whichever agent finds a ready, willing, and able buyer.

note A written statement acknowledging a debt and promising payment.

open-end mortgage A mortgage allowing the mortgagor to repay his loan before maturity without penalty or to refinance it.

open listing A listing given to an unlimited number of agents, and profiting only the agent directly responsible for the sale.

option The privilege, paid for with a small, forfeitable down payment, to buy a property at a given price within a given time.

origination fee A one-time charge that a lender levies for granting a mortgage.

perc test A test to determine the soil's drainage capacity, performed before the installation of a septic tank. Also called percolation test or soil percolation test.

personal property Anything not permanently attached to a house, such as freestanding bookshelves (as opposed to built-ins). Also called personalty. See *chattel*.

GLOSSARY

personal umbrella Insurance against losses beyond those covered by other policies. Also called umbrella liability.

points Service charges by a lending institution for giving a mortgage. One point is 1 percent of the amount of the loan.

prorate To distribute or divide (as obligations, money, etc.) proportionately.

purchase-money mortgage A mortgage granted to the buyer by the seller himself.

qualify a buyer To determine a potential buyer's financial position.

quitclaim deed A deed without warranties or covenants that conveys a seller's interest in or claim to a property.

real property Land and anything permanently attached to it, as a structure. Also called real estate.

Realtor A real-estate broker who belongs to the National Association of Realtors.

recording Filing documents, such as deeds and mortgage liens, in the public records, such as those kept at a county courthouse.

renegotiable/rollover mortgages Mortgages whose interest rates can be changed after a few years.

repair An alteration that "merely maintains your home in an ordinary, efficient operating condition. It doesn't add value to your home, or appreciably prolong its life" (IRS definition). It provides no tax benefit. See *improvement.*

replacement cost rider A guarantee that you will be reimbursed for the replacement cost of damaged goods without consideration of depreciation.

restriction A limitation on the use of a property, such as a zoning ordinance.

right of first refusal A potential buyer's right, granted by a seller, to match a third party's offer for a property.

right-of-way The right of one person or company to pass over or use another's land. Also, the land so used.

salesman In real estate, an agent who works for a broker.

secondary financing Funding secured by a junior mortgage.

second mortgage A mortgage supplementing a first mortgage. Also called second trust.

setback The distance, specified by municipal ordinance, from a building to the boundaries of its lot.

shared-appreciation mortgage A mortgage in which an investor provides financial aid to a homebuyer in return for a percentage of the home's growing value.

special assessment A property tax levied on only those property-holders who directly benefit from a specific municipal action, such as tying in their property to the city's sewer lines.

sump pump An automatic pump installed in a basement to pump out seeping groundwater.

survey A map of a tract of land showing its size, form, boundaries, improvements, elevation, and position relative to neighboring tracts.

tenancy by the entirety A form of property ownership by husband and wife in which, when one dies, the other automatically takes the title. Similar to joint tenancy.

tenancy in common A form of property ownership in which each owner has an undivided interest in the property. If one owner dies, his interest goes to his heirs, not to the other tenants in common.

"Time is of the essence" A phrase in a contract stipulating that the terms of the contract be performed by a specified date.

title Legal ownership, as evidenced by documents.

title defects Claims, liens, and similar drawbacks to a title.

title insurance Insurance against a loss incurred through defects of title.

title search An examination of title records, usually at the county courthouse, to determine a property's legal status and rightful owner.

GLOSSARY

Torrens system A system by which land is registered in some states, whereby title status and the like can be discovered without having to search public records further.

trust deed A deed conveyed by the seller to a third party to be held in trust pending the fulfillment of an obligation.

trustee A person or institution holding a property in trust for another. See *fiduciary*.

VA-insured or -guaranteed mortgage A home mortgage guaranteed by the Veterans Administration and available to eligible veterans.

valuation The estimated value of real property.

variance An exception to observance of a zoning ordinance, granted by a municipal body in response to specific needs.

warranty deed A deed affirming that the seller will protect a title transferred to a buyer against claimants.

wraparound mortgage A mortgage that covers the seller's old mortgage, with its low interest rate, the balance being repaid at a current interest rate.

zoning ordinances A municipality's ordinances defining and limiting land use.

INDEX

A
Abstract of title, 153, 156
Acceleration clause, 15–16
Action Real Estate, 85, 88
Adjustable mortgage loan (AML), 13
Adjustable-rate mortgage (ARM), 13, 16
Advertisements, 92–95, 99–101
Agents' commissions, 23, 27, 29–30, 63, 79–81, 85–88, 102, 133, 142, 174, 181
alChalabi, Margery, 111, 117
Ali, Masroor, 120
Allen, Charles, 180
AMC Home Inspection & Warranty Service, 163
American Association of Retired People, 202
American Institute of Architects, 123
American Institute of Real Estate Appraisers, 77
American Land Development Association, 177, 181, 183
American Society of Home Inspectors, 138
Andrews, Julie, 104
Appraisers, 76–77, 90
Architects, 119–127
Aronfy, Andrew G., 121
Assumable mortgage, 9, 92, 94
Attics, 189

B
Babcock, Richard F., 110–115, 117–118
Baldwin, Leo, 202, 204–206
Balloon mortgage, 20–21, 172

Basements, 72, 188
Bates, Robert C., 152, 157
Bathrooms, 71, 188
Beale, Calvin L., 110, 114, 118
Becker, William, 87
Bedrooms, 189
Better Business Bureau, 124, 172, 180
Bibler, Lester D., 203
Binders, 35, 38–39, 81–84, 139–140
Blend mortgage, 23
Bond, Robert J., 26, 30, 32
Boys Club, 103
Brandwein, Andrew, 84
Brandwein, Lillian, 84
Brenner, George H., 70
Broadbent, William R., 142
Brokers' contracts, 80–81
Brookings Institution, 3, 6, 110
Brooks, Michael P., 110, 113–115
Browdy, Sol, 120
Building the Dream, 7
Burger, Warren, 158
Butler, Samuel, 76
Buy-down, 23
Buyer-brokers, 141–143
Buyer qualification, *96,* 97, 132

C
California Real Estate Practice, 26
Campbell, Rex R., 113
Cape Cod style, 134
Capital-gains exclusion, 22
Capital-gains tax, 22, 62–63, 66, 74, 78, 169

Page numbers in italics refer to Exhibits.

INDEX

Caputo, David A., 113, 115, 117
Carter, John (pseud.), 25–26, 33
Case Western Reserve, 208
Certified financial statement, 19
Cesspools, 193, 195
Chase Econometrics, 206
Chase Manhattan Bank, 206
Chicago Title Insurance Company, 152, 155, 157
"Christina's World," 102
Cisney family, the, 103
Cities, best-, worst-managed, 116
Cities, future prospects, *109*
Closing costs, 145–158, 181; *see also* Settlement charges; Settlement statement
Clurman, David, 181, 183
College of Insurance, 41
Colonial style, 133
Colorado Department of Public Health, 194
Commissions. *See* Agents' commissions
Commuting, 4, 6, 130
Comparatives, 90
Comparing condo or co-op units, *171*
Comparing houses, *136–137*
Comparing mortgage offers, *16*
Comparing properties, *91*
Comparison of homeowners insurance policies, *42–43*
Condominiums, 6, 11, 23, 42, 59, 167–174, 182
Connoisseur, 104
Consumer's Union, 156, 158
Continental Real Estate Consultants, 86
Contractors, 26, 119–127
Contractors' payment schedule, 126
Cooperatives, 59, 167–174
Costs of running a house, 4
Creative financing, 7, 9, 19–23, 79, 100, 102; *see also* Mortgages
Creative selling, *103*

Credit unions, 17
Crittenden, Alan, 14
Cunningham, James V., 114–116
Custom-built houses, 119–127

D
Dawes, Jamie, 104
Deductibles, 53, 125
DeLaurentiis, Dino, 104
Department of Agriculture, 110, 200
Department of Commerce, 14
Department of Housing and Urban Development, 45, 152
Detached houses, 6
Dickinson, Peter A., 203, 205, 209
Direct-mail campaigns, 103
Discount brokers, 87–88
Distribution box, 196
Doherty, Joseph B., 162
Dommel, Paul R., 110, 114, 117
Down payment, 10–11, 14, 16, 19, 26
Downs, Anthony, 3–8
Drainage field, 194–199
Driveways, 185
Ducks Unlimited, 104
Due-on-sale clause, 9–10, 21–23, 92
Duplexes, 6

E
Earthquake insurance, 45
Edgar, R.A., 176, 179
Eldridge, Thomas R., 80
Electricity, 190
Elizabethan style, 134
Emlen, Alan L., 161
Energy-saving devices, 60–62, 70
Energy-saving tax credits, *61*
Equifax Services, 41
Escrow, 16–17
Escrow account, 15, 20
Escrow agent, 152
Escrow fund, 172
Estimated selling price, 70
Ewing, J.R., 111

INDEX

Exchanging houses, 62
Exclusive agency, 80
Exclusive right to sell, 80, 102

F
Fact sheet, model, *93*
Faulkner, John, 99–100
Federal Home Loan Mortgage Association (Freddie Mac), 17
Federal Housing Administration, 11, 18, 124, 167
Federal Insurance Administration, 45
Federal National Mortgage Association (Fannie Mae), 17, 21
Federal Trade Commission, 181
Financing, 7, 9–23, 90, 92, 181
Fireplaces, 72, 188
First-time buyers, 4
Fixed-rate mortgage, 11–14, 16, 21, 29
Floaters, 44, 56–57
Floating-rate mortgage, 11–16
Flood insurance, 45
Floors, 189
Forbes, 180
Ford, Gerald, 104
Ford, Henry II, 104
Ford, Kristina, 107, 113–115
Ford, Norman D., 202–203, 205
Foreclosure, 19–22
For Sale By Owner, 79
For-sale-by-owner agencies, 86
4-3-2-1 Realty, 86
Fribush, Ellis M., 15, 17, 19

G
Gahr, William N., 194
Gaines, Kenneth S., 30
Galfand, Alfred, 135
Garages, 186, 188
General Motors, 103
Godell, Chester, 179
Goldstone, Sidney, 124
Goode, John, 153
Goodwill Industries, 99
Gore, Mary, 86

Government Printing Office, 196
Graduated-payment mortgage (GPM), 12
Grease trap, 196
Ground lease, 22
Growing equity mortgage, 14
Guide to Public Services, 156

H
Haberle, Joan, 27, 29, 87
Haggling, 35–39
Hannafin, Jeanne, 31
Hansen, Lowell H., 119–120
Hansen, Niles, 114–115, 117
Hard-to-sell houses, 99–104
Harrison, Henry S., 134
Harrison, Roger, 13
Harvard-MIT Joint Center for Urban Studies, 5
Hayes, Donald R., 202, 207
Heating, 190–191
Hesseltine, H. Close, 202, 208
Hoffman, Norman, 41–42, 44–45, 53
Home-offices, 100
Homeowners insurance, 16, 21, 41–57
Homeowners tax exemption, 63, 66
Home Owners Warranty (HOW), 125
Homequity, 76
Homes. *See* Houses/homes
Home Sellers Center, 86
Homes International, 103
Home warranty, 138–139
Horowitz, Isaac, 202, 208
Horton, Elizabeth, 107
Household inventory, *46–52*
House inspectors, 138–139, 178, 185
Houses/homes
  as investments, 3–4, 7–8, 176
  Cape Cod, 134
  Colonial, 133
  costs of running, 4
  custom-built, 119–127
  exchanging, 62
  hard-to-sell, 99–104
  improvements checklist, *64–65*

225

INDEX

improvements to, 63–65, 69–74, 77–78, 100
luxury, 6, 101–102, 159–165
new vs. old, 133
prices of, 4
ranch, 5, 133–134
repairs to, 63, 100
second, 6, 56, 59–60, 62, 175–178, 181, 183–184, 204–205
split-entry, 134
split-level, 134
summer. *See* second
title to, 62–63
Tudor (Elizabethan), 134
unusual, 101–104, 161–162
vacation. *See* second
Houses: The Illustrated Guide to Construction, Design and Styles, 134
How to Be Your Own Lawyer—Sometimes, 80
How to Sell (and Buy) Your Home, 30
How to Sell Your House for More Than It's Worth, 75
Hudson Michael Realty, 161
Hunter, Robert, 152

I
Illustrated Properties, 161
Improvements checklist, *64–65*
Improvements, home, 63–65, 69–74, 77–78, 100
Improvements vs. repairs, *63*
Inflation escalators in title-insurance policies, 157
Installment contract, 22
Insurance
 comparison of homeowners policies, *42–43*
 earthquake, 45
 flood, 45
 homeowners, 16, 21, 41–57
 liability, 42
 life, 15
 limits on homeowners, *54*
 mortgage, 11, 16, 20–21
 mortgage life, 15
 private mortgage, 15, 23
 sleep, 45
 title, 152–158, 183
 workers' compensation, 45
Interest-rate indexes, 13–14, 16
Interval International, 183
Investments, houses as, 3–4, 7–8, 176
Iowa State University College of Design, 110
Irwin, Robert, 28–29, 31

J
James, Jesse, 126
J.K. Lasser's Your Income Tax, 59–60

K
Kantrowitz, Walter, 80
Kass, Benny L., 31–32
Kay, Jane Holtz, 112, 116
Kennedy estate, 104
Kerin, Ken, 7
Kerr, Andrew D. Jr., 202
King, Neil, 161
Kinne, A. Smith, 201, 203
Kitchens, 70–71, 188
Klein, Emanuel, 121
Koch, Edward I., 115

L
Ladies' Home Journal, 123
Lambert, Gerard B., 38
Landsman, Ron, 157
Laski, Harold J., 163
Lauber, Daniel, 111, 115
Lawyers Title Insurance Corporation, 153–155
Lease-option, 22
Lee, Thomas, 11, 23
Leisure Hour, 79
Leung, Albert S., 180
Liability insurance, 42
Life insurance, 15
Lindbergh baby, 189
Loan fees, 16
Loan-origination fees, 15, 158
Loeb, William, 205, 208–209
Lots, 124, 185
Lumpkin, Joseph H., 71

Luxury houses, 6, 101–102, 159–165

M
Macris, Dean L., 107
Macris, Marjorie, 107
Maher, Alice, 86
Mangan, W. Fred, 160
Manual of Septic Tank Practice, 196
Martin, Dean, 104
Martin, Steve, 104
Massachusetts Institute of Technology, 11
McGregor, Gloria S., 108, 112, 114–115, 117
Medical Economics, 104
Merrill Lynch, 14, 157
Metzen, Jack, 160
Metropolitan Museum of Art, 164
Middleton family, the, 103
Miller, Henry S. Jr., 160
Miro, Joan, 165
Money, 180
Monthly mortgage payments, 18
Morrison-Knudson Company, 108
Mortgage Guaranty Insurance Corporation, 20–21
Mortgage insurance, 11, 16, 20–21; *see also* Private mortgage insurance
Mortgage life insurance, 15
Mortgages, 4, 7, 9–23; *see also* Creative financing
 adjustable-rate, 13, 16
 assumable, 9, 92, 94
 balloon, 20–21, 172
 blend, 23
 comparing offers, *16*
 fixed-rate, 11–14, 16, 21, 29
 floating-rate, 11–16
 graduated-payment, 12
 growing equity, 14
 monthly payments, 18
 purchase-money, 21–22
 renegotiable, 13
 rollover, 13, 172
 second, 19–22
 shared-appreciation, 14
 sleeping second, 22
 wraparound, 22
Multiple listings, 80–81, 85–86, 88
Municipal health departments, 194–195
Municipal services, 129
Murr, C. Daniel, 141, 143

N
National Association of Home Builders, 124–125
National Association of Public Insurance Adjusters, 53
National Association of Real Estate Brokers, 79
National Association of Realtors, 7, 27, 31*n*, 80, 134, 139, 162
National Home Improvement Council, 124
National Insurance Consumer Organization, 152
National Register of Historic Places, 165
Nationwide Real Estate Inspectors Service, 160, 162–163
Neighborhoods, 33, 70, 129–131, 160–161, 176–177
 inspection checklist, *131*
Nelson, Judith, 97
Nevada State Real Estate Commission, 31
New houses vs. old, 133
New Jersey Real Estate Commission, 27, 32, 87
Newman, Paul, 164
New Yorker, The, 104
New York Mets, 160
New York State Department of Health, 199
New York Times, The, 180
New York University Graduate School of Public Administration, 107
New York University School of Continuing Education and Extension Services, 87
Nixon, Richard M., 104, 168

INDEX

Nondisturbance clause, 183
Novak, Kim, 104

O
O'Dea, Thomas L., 12
Office-condos, 173
Old houses vs. new, 133
Open listing, 80

P
"Pair and set" clause, 44
Park, Bob, 88
Parsons, Evelyn L., 202
Payson, Joan Whitney, 160
Peckovich, Nick, 162
Pennington, Jerry, 75
Percolation test, 195, 197
Performance bond, 122
Personal umbrella policy, 45
Petrowsky, Joseph L., 142
Picasso, Pablo, 165
Planned unit development (PUD), 168-169
Planning/Communications, 111
Plumbing, 191-192
Points, 15-16
Pomeroy, John H., 200
Post, John, 203-204
Preminger, Otto, 104
Prepayment penalty, 16, 92, 158
Pretnar, Tom, 161
Previews, 38, 95, 101-104, 161, 164
Price, Irving, 88, 161
Price, Sherman, 189
Prices, house, 4
Private mortgage insurance, 15, 23; *see also* Mortgage insurance
Probate costs, 182
Professional Builder, 70, 72
Property taxes, 15-16
Proposal to Purchase Memorandum, *82-83*
Protect Yourself in Real Estate, 28
Proxmire, William, 155
Public Adjuster, 53
Public Health Service, 196

Purchase-money mortgage, 21-22
Pyle, Jack I., 27

R
Ragatz, Richard L., 180-181, 184
Ranch style, 5, 133-134
Raphael, Stephen M., 182
Reagan, Ronald, 94, 104
Real Estate Research Corporation, 111
Real Estate Settlement Procedures Act (RESPA), 152
Real Estate Today, 27-28, 32
Redman family, the, 103
Region of country, 70
Reich, Larry, 111, 113, 117
Reissue rate, 153
Renegotiable mortgage, 13
Renting, 22-23, 42, 60, 66, 175-177, 182-183, 204
Repairs, home, 63, 100
Replacement cost rider, 44
Report of title, 153
Resort Condominiums International, 183
Retirement, 201-209
  best and worst states to retire to, *206-207*
Riders, 44
Rinzler, Harvey, 126
Rogers, Kenny, 104
Rollover mortgage, 13, 172
Ronson Company, 73
Roofs, 187
Rutgers Center for Urban Policy Research, 3, 107

S
Sakson, John, 32
Savings and loan associations, 10, 13, 17, 20, 77, 90
Schlaifer, Alan, 181
Schools, 77, 129-130
Schultz, Fred G., 75
Science Digest, 107
Sears, 157
Seasons, 77

INDEX

Second homes, 6, 56, 59–60, 62, 175–178, 181, 183–184, 204–205
Second mortgage, 19–22
Securities, 19
Seilheimer, Charles H. Jr., 6, 101–102, 104, 161–162
Seldin, Stephen, 81, 84, 126, 158, 167, 169
Septic tanks, 32, 178, 192–200
Settlement charges, lenders estimate of, *146–147; see also* Closing costs
Settlement statement, 148–151
Shared-appreciation mortgage, 14
Shearson/American Express, 157
Sheridan, Leo J. Jr., 72–73
Siding, 72, 186
Sikorski, Eugene, 179
Sleeping second mortgage, 22
Sleep insurance, 45
Smith, Al, 170
Smith, Henry E., 186, 188–189
Smith, Jeanette, 177, 183
Smith, Peter J., 199
Snowden, George Jr., 79
Society of Real Estate Appraisers, 77
Sotheby Parke Bernet International Realty Corporation, 6, 101–104, 161, 164
Split-entry style, 134
Split-level style, 134
State departments of consumer affairs, 172
State insurance commissions, 156–157
Sternlieb, George, 3, 6, 107
Stewart, Jimmy, 104
Stoker, Bruce, 4
Streisand, Barbra, 168
Stuart, Gilbert, 38
Suburban Home Advisors, 86
Suburbs, 6
Summer homes. *See* Second homes
Supreme Court, 10, 155
Surveys, 158, 178

T
Tax credits, 60–62
Tax deductions, 14, 59–65, 126, 169, 173
Taxes, 59–65, 70, 73–74, 130
Time-sharing, 7, 176, 179–184
most popular destinations, *182*
Title insurance, 152–158, 183
Title to house, 62–63
Torrens system, 153
Townhouses, 6
Treasury obligations, 12–13
Tudor style, 134
Turoff, Murray, 107

U
Unique Homes, 104
United States Department of Agriculture. *See* Department of Agriculture
United States Department of Commerce, *See* Department of Commerce
United States Department of Housing and Urban Development. *See* Department of Housing and Urban Development
United States Treasury obligations, 12–13
Unusual houses, 101–104, 161–162

V
Vacation homes. *See* Second homes
"Valued" policy coverage, 44
Verex Assurance, 20
Veterans Administration, 10, 18

W
Wagner, Alvin L. Jr., 77
Waivers of lien claims, 122
Waldorf, Paul, 163
Walls, 190
Ward, William J., 122, 186
Warkentin, Dan B., 141
Warranty, home, 138–139
Weather, 202–203

INDEX

Wennerstrom, Bruce, 101–102
Where to Retire on a Small Income, 202
White, Stanford, 94
Wickstrum, Bart K., 76
Wiederhorn, Rick, 112–114, 118
Wiesel, Carl, 207–209
Williams, Harlan C., 72–73
Wilton, Charles, 79
Windows, 189
Woodward, Joanne, 164

Workers' compensation insurance, 45
Worldwatch Institute, 4
Wraparound mortgage, 22
Wright, Frank Lloyd, 119, 123
Wright, Gwendolyn, 7
Wyeth, Andrew, 102

Z

Zilavy, Dennis L., 86–88
Zoning laws, 129

OTHER TITLES OF RELATED INTEREST FROM MEDICAL ECONOMICS BOOKS

Designing and Building Your Own Professional Office
Murray Schwartz, D.D.S.
ISBN 0-87489-228-7

Insurance Strategies for Physicians
Phillips Huston
ISBN 0-87489-279-1

Personal Money Management for Physicians, Third Edition
Lawrence Farber
ISBN 0-87489-253-8

Tax Strategy for Physicians, Second Edition
Lawrence Farber
ISBN 0-87489-258-9

ABCs of Investing Your Retirement Funds, Second Edition
C. Colburn Hardy
ISBN 0-87489-259-7

The Beginning Investor, Second Edition
Philip Harsham
ISBN 0-87489-365-8

For information, write to:
Customer Service Manager
MEDICAL ECONOMICS BOOKS
Oradell, New Jersey 07649

Or dial toll-free: 1-800-223-0581, ext. 2755
(Within the 201 area: 262-3030, ext. 2755)